Espoused to Christ

Praise for *Espoused to Christ*

"Though Erin has called this a theology of consecrated virginity, this work is more than a theological treatment of this topic. It also contains her personal sharing of aspects of the lived reality of this vocation espoused to Christ. This book delves deep into many, perhaps even most, aspects of the life of the consecrated virgin, making it a good resource for understanding what constitutes this vocation and the importance of its presence in the Church. It will be useful for those discerning the call to consecrated virginity and for those within the local Church who are responsible for accompanying them in their formation."

—**Bishop William McGrattan,** Diocese of Calgary

"With a mixture of historical background, theological reflection, and insights from personal experience, this book explores consecrated virginity in ways that are profound and practical. A must-read for anyone discerning or living this vocation or wishing to understand it better."

—**Bishop Daniel Miehm,** Diocese of Peterborough

"Beautiful and profound!"

—**Fr. Mark Goring, C.C.,** Pastor, St. Mary's Parish, Ottawa

"*Espoused to Christ* is a carefully researched and documented presentation of consecrated virginity. It is enriched with many personal insights from the author, who lives this vocation herself. I highly recommend this brilliant, informative, engaging book not only for women discerning this vocation but also for those simply interested in this little-known form of consecrated life."

—**Anna Hecold,** Consecrated Virgin and Formator,
Archdiocese of Toronto

"As someone with thirty years of experience in the formation and accompaniment of women discerning the vocation to consecrated virginity in the Archdiocese of Toronto, I deeply appreciate this book. Erin offers rich and varied resources in a way that is scholarly yet also very accessible. I would add this book to the list of required reading for those in formation and recommend it to all consecrated virgins for the ongoing deepening in and appropriation of their vocation."

—**Mary Bastedo, M.Div.,** Former Formator, Archdiocese of Toronto

"A deeply insightful exploration of consecrated virginity, this book illuminates its rich history, spiritual significance, and enduring relevance, especially for women discerning this very special vocation."

—**Josephine Lombardi,** Assistant Dean and Associate Professor, St. Augustine's Seminary; Author, *On Earth as It Is in Heaven*

"This book is truly remarkable. A profound and deeply spiritual masterpiece, it illuminates the richness and depth of the vocation of consecrated virginity. With remarkable theological insight and the depth of her own lived witness, Erin Kinsella masterfully weaves together an integrated and compelling exploration of this sacred calling. Having ministered to young people in their vocational discernment for decades, I recognize this book as an invaluable resource. It will undoubtedly inspire many hearts to embrace the dignity and beauty of Jesus' call to be His—as a consecrated virgin."

—**Angèle Regnier,** Cofounder, Catholic Christian Outreach

"I welcome this book because it both uses a theological lens and addresses several particular aspects of this vocation."

—**Crystal Hampson,** Consecrated Virgin, Diocese of Saskatoon

"Thoroughly researched, theologically rich, engaging, and accessible, this welcome book provides invaluable insight into the history, beauty, and meaning of consecrated virginity. Balancing spiritual depth with practical wisdom, Erin Kinsella's writing shines with sincerity, joy, and love for the Divine Bridegroom and His beloved Bride, the Church."

—**Dr. Christina Labriola,** Consecrated Virgin, Archdiocese of Toronto

Erin Kinsella

ESPOUSED TO CHRIST

A Theology of Consecrated Virginity

SOPHIA INSTITUTE PRESS
Manchester, New Hampshire

Cover design by LUCAS Art & Design, Jenison, MI.

On the cover: lily photo by Adrian Dale, https://unsplash.com/photos/a-white-flower-with-a-long-stem-NEAKOl_xHXE.

Nihil obstat: Most Reverend Yvan Mathieu, SSL, PhD, *Censor deputatus*
Archdiocese of Ottawa-Cornwall, April 9, 2025

Imprimatur: Most Reverend Marcel Damphousse, Archbishop of Ottawa-Cornwall,
Ottawa, Ontario, April 10, 2025

Sophia Institute Press
Box 5284, Manchester, NH 03108
1-800-888-9344

www.SophiaInstitute.com

Sophia Institute Press® is a registered trademark of Sophia Institute.

paperback ISBN 979-8-88911-530-4
ebook ISBN 979-8-88911-531-1

Library of Congress Control Number: 2025935193

First printing

SPA POD 2025

This book is dedicated to Lorenzo and Nico.
You teach me more about the love of the Father
than I could ever read in books.

It is also dedicated to Sr. Dianne.
Thank you for the beautiful witness
of your consecrated life …
and for teaching me what a split infinitive is.

Lastly, it is dedicated to Mom, Dad, Kelly, and Dave.
I'm so grateful for your love and for the gift of our family.

Contents

Foreword

The 1963 Constitution on the Sacred Liturgy *Sacrosanctum Concilium* was responsible for some of the most visible and widely recognized effects of the Second Vatican Ecumenical Council. But amid all the directives on the various liturgical reforms, paragraph 80 contains one unassuming line:

> The rite for the consecration of virgins at present found in the Roman Pontifical is to be revised.

On the surface, this looks like a simple call to revise one ritual among many others to be similarly revised as part of the mission of the Council. Yet this particular revision was, in actuality, far more radical than a simple update. While most of the revisions called for by *Sacrosanctum Concilium* pertained to familiar and routine parts of Catholic life at the time, the revision of the ancient ritual for the consecration of virgins did something a bit more "outside the box": it effectively reintroduced to the lived reality of the modern Church the earliest form of consecrated life, which had been all but popularly forgotten.

The ancient Ordo Virginum is the earliest precursor to religious life properly so called as we know it today; thus, it shares the core values of a life lived according to the evangelical counsels, including, among other things, a closer following of Christ in His own chosen way of life, a public witness, and a call to live as an eschatological sign of the "life of the world to come."

At the same time, consecrated virginity is also a "new" vocation structured around a very different canonical paradigm. Unlike religious, consecrated virgins are consecrated passively by their bishops after stating a resolve to persevere in their holy way of life, rather than actively professing vows in a kind of "contract" with the Church as represented by a religious superior; they are consecrated individually by their bishops and tied to a particular local church rather than to a religious institute that may minister across many dioceses; and consecrated virgins are not specifically called to a common life necessarily involving a shared residence, participation in corporate apostolates, or community devotional practices.

Due to their very nature, most religious communities essentially grew from the ground up, originating in the charismatic gifts of a founder or foundress who provided a concrete vision for the life, formation, and mission of their spiritual sons and daughters. Speaking in very broad terms, the task of the institutional Church in these cases was and is one of prudent discernment, curating the religious charism in such a way that unhelpful elements were pruned and appropriate canonical structures were overlaid or applied to the communities' lived understanding of their identity.

But the Ordo Virginum of today is developing according to almost an opposite dynamic. The Church has already given us the law and canonical structure for this form of consecrated life, but since we have no founder (or rather, we might say the Church herself is our foundress!), we are still growing in our understanding of how this vocation should look in all its practical manifestations in daily life.

The challenge is to discern how to live as consecrated virgins—and, in turn, how to form future consecrated virgins—as radical witnesses as fervent religious, but in a way fully appropriate to our own unique vocation.

One mistake to be avoided is the temptation to use religious life as the standard measure by which to judge the Ordo Virginum, whether in treating consecrated virginity as a "watered down" form of religious life or seeking to graft distinctively monastic customs onto the life of nonmonastic consecrated virgins in ways that are pastorally inappropriate.

On the other hand, it would be just as problematic, if not more so, if we were to regard the consecration of virgins as being akin to a simple private commitment that did not obligate the newly consecrated to anything more than the basic Christian virtue required of all Catholics. Not only does this run plainly contrary to the mind of the Church, but it would not be conducive to the spiritual flourishing of consecrated virgins themselves, and it would deprive the people of God of the great gift that the restored Ordo Virginum has the potential to be when lived fully and well.

Collectively, there is still a great deal of work to be done on many levels, from scholarly to popular. There are still many open technical theological and canonical questions about the Ordo Virginum. And, at least in the English-speaking world, most dioceses are just starting to develop formation programs and practical policies for the care of local consecrated virgins.

Certainly, at this point, no one work can do it all or answer all the questions. But in this book, Erin Kinsella has a made a laudable and much-needed start.

In combining theology with her own lived experience, Erin presents some of the foundational themes of a call to consecrated virginity to those discerning and being formed in this vocation.

These themes, while, of course, not answering every question that could possibly be asked, nevertheless serve as an essential foundation for consecrated virgins' continued personal growth in their God-given call and identity.

In particular, the understanding of the role of the Cross in the life of Christ's brides and the right of the faithful to the spiritual maternity of a consecrated virgin present the "rich soil" (see Matt. 13:8) needed for those of us in the Ordo Virginum to bear fruit in our vocation and truly to become, in a real sense, as St. Cyprian described, the "the flower of the tree that is the Church."

Jenna Cooper
Consecrated virgin

Preface

The material in this book comes from a retreat I gave to candidates for Consecrated Virginity Lived in the World.[1] During my own formation, which took place largely before *Ecclesiae Sponsae Imago*[2] came out, there was not a lot of material available that spoke to consecrated virginity specifically, though, of course, there is a vast amount regarding consecrated life in general. This book will, I hope, be helpful for consecrated virgins, those forming them, those being formed to receive the consecration, and anyone who is interested in learning more about the vocation. Concepts are supported with many quotes from Church Fathers and writings of various popes and saints. Readers are highly encouraged to go

1 Note: Though Consecrated Virginity Lived in the World is the proper name of the vocation (with the rite being called "The Rite of Consecration of a Virgin Living in the World"), for the purposes of this document I'll use the term consecrated virginity in its place for the sake of simplicity. If at any time I'm referring to consecrated virginity *not* lived in the world, which specifies cloistered nuns who receive the consecration of virgins, I will specifically note that in the text.

2 Congregation for Institutes of Consecrated Life and Societies of Apostolic Life, *Ecclesiae Sponsae Imago: Instruction on the Ordo Virginum*, (Libreria Editrice Vaticana, 2018).

to the original sources, especially the ones cited frequently, to read the documents in their entirety. They are treasures of grace and you will likely find that reading the quotes within the context they are taken from gives an added richness.

With respect to the approach I've taken with the material, it was imperative to look back to the beginnings of the Church, in what is contained in Holy Scripture, in the witness of the first consecrated virgins, and in the teachings of the early Church Fathers, since this was the first origin and context of consecrated virginity. However, we now have more than two thousand years of theological deepening in the Church's understanding of virginity, Mariology, ecclesiology, consecrated life, the meaning of the body, marriage, and many other areas. I've tried to "read" consecrated virginity in a way that is faithful to its expressions in the early Church, but through the various lenses afforded by theological deepening.

The reader will certainly notice some overlap between chapters. The gift (and challenge) of looking back to our beginnings while allowing the theology that has since unfolded to interpenetrate all these foundations doesn't give rise to easily discrete categories. We sometimes say that our Faith is like a seamless garment—everything is woven together, and what we believe about Christ impacts what we believe about Mary, and what we believe about Mary impacts what we believe about holy virginity, and so on. The overlap between chapters is part of understanding the bigger picture and how all things fit together.

Practically speaking, even as we're looking at these theological developments, there are applied aspects of consecrated virginity that the worldwide Church is grappling with. The publication of *Ecclesiae Sponsae Imago* was a watershed moment for the life of this vocation in the modern Church, but it only came out in

2018—very recently. Before its release, dioceses were extremely varied in terms of formation programs for consecrated virginity. Some bishops were extremely proactive in making the vocation known in their dioceses, while others were somewhat unaware of the vocation altogether, or didn't understand it well. Presently there are norms given in *Ecclesiae Sponsae Imago* regarding formation, and many dioceses have solid formation programs in place, even though there is still wide variability between dioceses. Even so, it is inevitable that additional resources and Church documents will appear in the coming years as Rome sees the need for greater clarity in the theological or practical norms that *Ecclesiae Sponsae Imago* has laid out.

One simple example of this is the indication of an optional veil imposition during the consecration Mass. Some bishops have suggested this was an error and was only listed as optional because it's optional in the consecration of virgins *not* living in the world (i.e. nuns who can receive a different form of the consecration). Those nuns would already be wearing a religious habit and therefore the veil would be impractical, and it was thus indicated in the rite as optional, and from this they argue that the veil *should* be mandatory in the Rite of Consecration of a Virgin Living in the World because of its symbolism. This is a small example, but it illustrates the reality that we are likely to see these kinds of things (and even more important issues) clarified in greater degrees.

A practical note about reading this book: theological study is always at the service of love. As you read, my prayer is that it's the love of the Divine Bridegroom that you more deeply discover. I would encourage you, as you read, to note any points that present a consolation or a resistance in your heart. By consolation, I mean (in the words of St. Ignatius of Loyola) anything by which your soul "comes to be inflamed with love of its Creator and

Lord."[3] By resistance, I mean any time you feel an inner push back, discomfort, or lack of peace regarding something that you've just read. Take these consolations and resistances to prayer; the Lord will likely have something to say about them. At the end of each chapter, I'll also note some suggested Scripture passages to pray with that are related to the material just covered.

Finally, to my dear sisters of the Ordo Virginum,[4] what a gift it is to be living this vocation! My prayer for all of us is that we might fall more in love with Jesus every day and become the saints He is calling us to be, each in our little corner of the world. Please pray for me—I pray for you daily.

3 Ignatius of Loyola, "Rules for Perceiving the Movements Caused in the Soul: First Week," *The Spiritual Exercises*, accessed July 7, 2024, https://mycatholic.life/books/the-spiritual-exercises-of-saint-ignatius-of-loyola/rules/.

4 Ordo Virginum is the traditional Latin translation for the Order of Virgins, which includes all those who have received the Consecration of a Virgin Living in the World.

1

The Nature and Practicalities of Vocation and Commitment

As a treasure of inestimable value that God pours into clay vessels (cf. 2 Cor 4:7), this vocation is truly an undeserved gift. It encounters the person in her actual humanity, always in need of redemption and yearning for the full meaning of her existence. It finds its origin and dynamic centre in the grace of God, who unceasingly acts with the tenderness and the strength of his merciful love in the often complex and sometimes contradictory events of human life, helping the person to grasp her uniqueness and the unity of her being, enabling her to make a total gift of self.[5]

The Nature of Vocation as Call and Covenant

What is always the first sentence that comes in every vocations presentation? This: vocation comes from the Latin word *vocare*, which is "to call." We speak of love as a movement where there is a lover, a beloved, and the movement of love that is shared between them. This is why love follows after the reality of God, who

[5] *Ecclesiae Sponsae Imago*, no. 88.

is love; it is a reality of God the lover, Christ the beloved, and the Holy Spirit who is the love shared between them in what is called *perichoresis*, a kind of "dance" of interpenetrating love between the Persons of the Trinity.

Vocations can also be seen in this dynamic with the Holy Trinity as lover, us as the beloved, and vocation as the "being-ness" which is the fruit of that relationship. God calls us into relationship with Him, and into what Vatican II calls the universal vocation to holiness, and this constitutes the primary vocation of all Christians. It's from this universal vocation that our particular vocation comes as a deepening of our relationship with God. We hear the call to a vocation through the deepening of our vocation to holiness, and our vocation deepens our ability to live our call to holiness. This is also why those who have the challenge of living in the single life in a permanent way are not excluded from having a vocation even if their call might not include a particular vocation. The reality of a vocation to single life, in terms of whether it exists and what would characterize it, is still something the Church is coming to understand, but this is a question for another time!

A vocation is also a covenantal relationship. In the Old Testament, we see contractual agreements where one person trades a good or service for money or for another good or service, but we also see covenants that are made. God makes a covenant with Noah after the flood to assure Man that He will never send another flood; with Abraham to give him descendants and land and blessing; with Moses when God gave him the law that governed the people Israel; with David when He promises a descendent who would sit on the throne and secure the promises made to Abraham; with the people through the prophets promising deliverance from sin; and ultimately (and most definitively) through the covenant established in Christ for the forgiveness of sins and the salvation of Man.

Covenants, as Scott Hahn points out in *A Father Who Keeps His Promises*, is not an exchange of goods or services, but an exchange of persons.[6] It is constituted by a reciprocal self-donation between God and Man. And we participate in the covenant established definitively in Christ through hearing our call to vocation, receiving it as a gift from God—and, ultimately, as God's self-donation to us—and giving ourselves to Him without holding anything back.

When I was discerning my own vocation, I did a retreat with the Sisters of Life, and they made the point that our vocation is a gift that we receive from the Lord. They also pointed out that it's possible for us to have wounds or barriers that prevent us from freely receiving this gift and returning it in love to the Lord. At the time, it was so hard for me to hear, because I could feel the places in my own heart that were shielded over and protected in such a way that I knew, as they were speaking, that I wasn't able to freely receive the gift of my own vocation. Part of this was because of wounding experiences that I'd had in previous discernment of religious life, and I knew then that the Lord needed (and wanted!) to heal those places of my heart to be able to receive His love openly and without fear. Then, instead of my prayer being, "Lord, show me my vocation," it became, "Lord, open my heart to Your love." It was in this prayer that I experienced the healing that allowed Him to reveal my own heart to me and to show me how I was created to love Him and others. It was a very real experience of Him giving Himself to me so that I could offer myself fully to Him.

Thinking of a vocation in this way, as a self-donation in response to God's self-donation, it is not foundationally about what we *do*,

6 Scott Hahn, *A Father Who Keeps His Promises: God's Covenant Love in Scripture* (Servant, 1998), 26.

but who we *are* in Him. There can be a temptation to think that we must somehow earn our vocation, or merit it in some way. It's true that the various vocations have various ways that are intrinsic to living that vocation, for example a priest offers Mass and the other sacraments, and it would be a strange priesthood where those were not fundamental components of the priest's life, but these *doings* flow from *being*. I receive my identity from Christ, because God "fully reveals man to man himself and makes his supreme calling clear,"[7] and identity is never reduced to doing. The things that we do as part of the life of consecrated virginity flow from and confirm the identity of who we *are*. To be clear, the things that we do are extremely important, and our free choices are what constitute our character and virtue, but these are founded principally in grace and need to take their shape based on who we are in Christ. In other words, we cannot know what we ought to do before we know who we are, as John Paul II says in *A Theology of the Body*.[8] Our vocation places us in the heart of Christ in a particular mode of being from which comes all that we do.

I've had to learn this the hard way, because several years ago I developed a debilitating condition after a bike fall and went through the process of not being able to continue working and needing to move back to my parent's home in Ottawa. In light of my physical limitations, there are some days when I am simply

7 Vatican Council II, Pastoral Constitution on the Church in the Modern World *Gaudium et spes* (Joy and Hope) (December 7, 1965), no. 22, https://www.vatican.va/archive/hist_councils/ii_vatican_council/documents/vat-ii_const_19651207_gaudium-et-spes_en.html.

8 John Paul II, *Man and Woman He Created Them: A Theology of the Body*, trans. Michael Waldstein (Pauline Books & Media, 2006), no. 15.1.

unable to carry out some things in the rule of life I have adopted, through which I am committed to serving my Divine Bridegroom.

You may imagine how challenging and even frustrating this may be at times. For example, I may not feel well enough to attend daily Mass, to help my parish community as I desire to, or I may experience pain that hinders me from doing much more than simply giving myself to God as I am.

However, I have also asked myself these questions: Is a married couple any less married when they are sleeping? Is a bed-bound nun any less of a nun? Of course not, but this is a helpful reminder that throughout my life with Christ my vocation is not primarily "comprised" of my health condition, thoughts, feelings, or even what I do; but rather what is most essential about my vocation is who God is and His love for me—and who I am through, with, in, and for Him—who inspires and directs the "what I do"-ness in our relationship.

I somehow expected that I would be a different person after my consecration, more virtue-filled and less sin-inclined, and was genuinely perturbed by finding that I was the same me as the day before my consecration, even if who I am in Christ had been definitively confirmed by the Church. Jesus knows what He's getting Himself into when He gives Himself to us in this vocation, and He's not surprised by our weakness and inability to live it as we desire to. The important thing is this: we can always participate in a dynamism of self-gift, because the Lord always wants all of us, warts and all. He loves it when we give Him our whole selves with confidence that we are loved in our brokenness.

Part of the grace of the vocation is that we get to see ourselves as we really are. We can think of spouses who have just married and moved in with each other, and they quickly realize things about themselves in terms of their preferences, pet peeves, imperfections and wounds through this new closeness of the marriage bond.

Proverbs 27:17 says, "As iron sharpens iron, so one person sharpens another," and we know that wherever there is a relationship between persons, especially where that relationship is very deep, we help in the purification of each other. In the spousal relationship with Christ, the consecrated virgin can always know that when there are bumps or areas that need sharpening, it is always she who needs to be purified and sharpened, and this is a real gift. Then, we can do what St. Thérèse spoke of and throw ourselves into the merciful arms of Jesus a thousand times every day![9]

Another beautiful and foundational reality is that we belong to Christ's Mystical Body through our baptism in an irrevocable way. Our holiness and conformation to Christ, which deeply involves our vocation, since it constitutes who we are in Christ, comes through the gateway of baptism, and the life of grace in the soul is made possible through it. There is a great comfort in this because it means that our holiness does not rest on our merits or accomplishments, though it does require our cooperation with God, as we say with St. James, "I will show you my faith by my deeds" (2:18).

If we are in a covenantal relationship with God through our baptism and live out our vocation in a special way, we can be assured that God never holds Himself back from us. His self-gift is complete and unending. Since God *is* love, and because His self-gift is without limits (on His end, though we can try at times to shut the door on our end!), it means that there is no moment that God is not offering us the very depths of His faithful love and His *hesed*, His tender compassion. God cannot violate the covenant He establishes with us because He is unable to violate

[9] Letter of St. Thérèse to Abbé Maurice Bellière, June 21, 1897, https://carmelitequotes.blog/2021/03/28/therese-msc36v-audacity/.

His nature. His love and His self-gift are enduring, even if we fail and we fall, which we will.

The Reality of Vocation as Permission

There is a crisis of commitment in our culture that has seeped into Catholic culture. I can think of something as simple as trying to get teens to sign up for a retreat from when I was a youth minister. It was like pulling teeth, because they were often holding out to see if there were any "better" options that would come up; they truly lived in a real FOMO (fear of missing out). And then, in the day or two before the event, we would have waves of registrations as FOMO about the retreat kicked in!

This is a non-consequential example, but there are many things that are very consequential. Rates of marriage are falling, rates of bearing children are falling, divorce rates are climbing, job stability has changed significantly from what it once was, and the rate of change in culture has accelerated more in the last fifty years than in any other period in history. There is a general sense of unease in people, because, as a culture that is moving to become post-Christian, it is being built on constantly shifting sand, where trust is placed in things that cannot fulfill their promises and nothing of self-gift is demanded of the human person; the means of attaining true freedom and happiness are being buried.

The Gospel according to Matthew speaks to this:

> Therefore everyone who hears these words of mine and puts them into practice is like a wise man who built his house on the rock. The rain came down, the streams rose, and the winds blew and beat against that house; yet it did not fall, because it had its foundation on the rock. But everyone who hears these words of mine and does not put

> them into practice is like a foolish man who built his house on sand. The rain came down, the streams rose, and the winds blew and beat against that house, and it fell with a great crash (Matt. 7:24–27).

The only constant is Christ and the truths of the whole created order that are bound up in Him, but for a culture that is largely relativistic, everyone is at the beach building houses.

The Lord has such a personal way of bringing each of us to a place where we can commit to Him in a permanent way. In my own vocation journey, the Lord knew that to enter freely into this vocation of consecrated virginity I would need to know that I had discerned and ruled out other possible vocations. My spiritual director, after helping me rule out religious life, encouraged me to put on some makeup and some fancy clothes, go to a place where I knew there were good men my age, and simply be open to however the Lord wanted to move. Thinking back, he may have used "makeup and fancy clothes" as a general way of saying "do whatever helps you to feel good in your skin," but I literally went out and purchased makeup because I didn't own any. I went a number of times to a popular Catholic event that I had attended many times before, and which I knew many single Catholic men attended very regularly. While I was trying to be intentionally open, there was *not a single eligible man there*, and during that whole time, I felt like I was stepping out of *who* I was. I met again with my spiritual director, and we agreed that the Lord was clearly showing me that marriage was not my call either!

Some people have a very clear sense of what they're called to early in their vocational discernment. As I was going through the discernment process, I didn't experience that, and it was something that troubled me for awhile because I thought that I should have absolute, unwavering certainty before receiving the consecration. However, a priest friend of mine shared once that he experienced something similar, and he recounted how, coming to a point in his formation where he really had to commit, he thought to himself, "Will I come to the end of my life and regret choosing the priesthood?" He was honestly able to answer himself with a resounding, "No!" It made me look at my own call in a different way, and I could very easily say to the Lord that I would not come to the end of my life wishing that I hadn't responded to this call.

Additionally, I experienced several significant healings from the Lord, one being the one mentioned previously. These healings allowed me to receive my vocation as a gift, to entrust myself fully to the Lord and, with great freedom, to say yes to the deeper purification that vocational commitment brings. The Lord knew exactly what I needed to be free from in order to commit to Him in the form of consecrated virginity, just as He knows what each of us needs, different as those things may be.

A friend of mine who is a priest was giving a presentation to some young adults at a vocations conference, and he spoke so beautifully about overcoming the challenges of commitment, but even more about the freedom of commitment. Likely, for you who have come to this point in your discernment, you are committed to following the Lord's call (or are on the way to being able to give a full yes!). However, it's the freedom of commitment that I want to share. My priest friend shared that the entry into our vocations is both freeing and scary because it gives the Lord permission to work on the deep parts of us. When we give a definitive yes that is ratified by the Church, we give the Lord permission to dig into the deepest parts of our hearts, and the stability of our call, vocation, and relationship with Him is the firm ground that allows that to happen without us running (even if we may try at times).

If we think of this in terms of marriage, on the rocky days it's the vows that are pronounced that can be clung to—not the good feelings or even the action or inaction of the other person—it's the promise that was made before God that can be relied on to direct the continuation of commitment. The spouse can say, "I made this vow to you forever, my beloved, and I will trust that because I've made this vow and have not given myself the option of getting out of this relationship." How much more can we experience this with God, where the resolution is not made before God but with God Himself. When we give that definitive yes, we are giving a definitive yes to being made holy, to entering more deeply into that primary universal call to holiness.

We are encountering Christ more deeply, and though sometimes the word encounter is used in a flowery way, its roots mean "to go in against"; encountering Christ, though He is gentle and will not break the bruised reed (Isa. 42:3; Matt. 12:20), is a difficult thing because it brings us face to face with every broken and shame-filled recess of our hearts. It is not that Christ is harsh, because He is never anything but love, all the way through. The process itself can be harsh, however, because it changes a nature that is disordered and sets it to order. It also takes us to unexpected places (likely both interiorly and exteriorly!) because "no individual knows what his own holiness consists of."[10]

Commitment, both in Christ to us through His Church confirming our vocation and in us to Christ in responding to His call with our free *yes*, is the necessary security that He knows we need in order to be made into saints. This, in turn, gives us freedom because we know that God will never withdraw His gift of self

[10] Jacques Philippe, *In the School of the Holy Spirit*, trans. Helena Scott (Sceptre Publishers, 2007), 18.

from us, and also because we cannot betray ourselves by running when the process of sanctification is demanding. It's a gift to know that, even if I resist interiorly to some degree when God is doing something, the reality of who I am in Him is unchanging. In other words, it allows for my weakness and inconstancy to be present without invalidating our spousal union. What a beautiful gift!

One of my favorite readings from the Office is for the Saturday of the Sixteenth Week in Ordinary Time. St. John Chrysostom writes in his commentary on the Second Letter to the Corinthians, "For those who are loved enter fearlessly into the heart of their lover."[11] Everything resides in the heart of Christ—my worth and calling, my woundedness and healing, His invitation and my freedom to respond.

So, above all things the call is to enter deeply into the heart of Christ. All the components on our journey—meditations, Liturgy of the Hours, Mass, adoration, group sharing, individual direction, silence, rest—these are all ways that Jesus will draw us to Him. Hosea 11:4, speaking of how God pursues His chosen people Israel, even when they turn from Him again and again, says, "I will draw them with the cords of Adam, with the bands of love: and I will be to them as one that taketh off the yoke on their jaws: and I put his meat to him that he might eat." This is the Douay-Rheims translation, but I love that one because the "cords of Adam," sometimes translated as the "cords of Man" or the "cords of human kindness," ultimately speak to the way that God knows how to lead each of us. He knows the heart of Man—each of our hearts—and knows how to speak so that we can hear His voice, full of love for us.

[11] John Chrysostom, *Commentary on Second Corinthians,* trans. St. George Monastery, Monaxi Agapi and Anna Skoubourdis (Lulu Press, 2020), 24.

Questions and Scriptures for Reflection

1. Do I know that the Lord is unchanging? That His love is a firm foundation?

2. Are there places in my heart where I struggle to say yes to the Lord?

Isaiah 43:1
Jeremiah 29:11–14
Hosea 11:4
Song of Songs 4:9–11
Matthew 4:18–22
Matthew 7:24–27
John 20:11–16
2 Corinthians 4:7

2

History of Consecrated Virginity

When your charism came into being it did not take shape in accordance with specific ways of life. Rather, it was institutionalized little by little until it became a true and proper solemn, public consecration, conferred by the Bishop in an evocative liturgical rite which made the consecrated woman the sponsa Christi, an image of the Church as Bride.[12]

Roots of Virginity

Christianity's roots are in Judaism, so the history of consecrated virginity can also find roots there, though there were no direct models of it in Jewish life or in Greek or Roman cultures because perpetual virginity was largely seen as something undesirable. Interestingly, there was great importance given to virginity in Judaic practice, with the intent of women retaining their virginity until

12 Benedict XVI, Address to the Participants in the International Congress-Pilgrimage of the Ordo Virginum (the Order of Virgins) (May 15, 2008), https://www.vatican.va/content/benedict-xvi/en/speeches/2008/may/documents/hf_ben-xvi_spe_20080515_ordo-virginum.html.

the bond of marriage. There was an elaborate monetary system for dowries (e.g. double for the daughter of a priest, etc.) and for transgressions relating to rape (e.g. the rapist needed to pay the father of the victim to account for her "shame" and loss of value for future marriage). There were also regulations governing the signs that should be present on the wedding night of a virgin.

Marriage was seen as rooted in the command of Genesis to be fruitful and multiply, meaning that traditionally Jews entered marriage as an obedient and proper response to God's command. This also means, then, that unmarried women were not common and were seen at times as having been deprived of God's favor or even having committed sin that resulted in the punishment of remaining unmarried. It was considered dishonourable to remain unmarried, especially for women. We can see this epitomized in the book of Judges where Jephthah's daughter "bewailed her virginity on the mountains" (see Judg. 11:38, NRSVCE).

There *is* a kind of echo of consecrated life in the Old Testament in those who were Nazirites. Nazirites were considered "consecrated to the LORD" (Num. 6:8) and made vows to abstain from wine and grape products, not to cut their hair, and not to make themselves unclean by contact with a corpse. Samson and Samuel are examples of people mentioned as having taken a vow as a Nazirite. Nazirite itself means "consecrated" or "separated." Nazirites could be men or women, and permanent or temporary. They became Nazirites by intentional verbal declaration, which could even include saying "me too" as a Nazirite passed by.[13]

Unless they declared they were Nazirites forever or for all their lives, the vow was considered to be thirty days (unless specified

[13] See Mishneh Torah, "Nazir," accessed July 15, 2024, https://www.sefaria.org/Mishnah_Nazir.3?lang=bi, 1.

for longer than thirty days but less than forever).[14] The end of a Nazirite vow came about by offering a burnt offering, sin offering, and peace offering at the Temple at the end of the declared time period,[15] but, after the fall of the physical Temple, a person would be considered a perpetual Nazirite because there was no physical temple in which to offer the required offerings.[16] A Nazirite also shaved their head/cut their hair as a symbol of the conclusion of their vow. Those with proper authority over the Nazirite (e.g. father over daughter, husband over wife) had the ability to annul the vow.[17] We can see the meaning of Nazirite vows in the penitential practice, the public declaration, the authority over the declaration, and the association with the Temple as a kind of "type" for what we see in what becomes Christian consecrated life. However, it's important to note that Nazirites were not required to be virgins or unmarried, or remain in this state, so there are also obvious differences, and we should not understand a Nazirite vow to be a direct precursor to consecrated life.

In the time immediately preceding Christ, and during His life, there was a sect of Judaism called the Essenes. They likely lived a kind of communal, monastic lifestyle in Qumran, and likely practiced celibacy to some extent.[18] Their motive for celibacy was partly to quell sexual urges, even to the point of rejecting marriage for fear that they could become ritually impure if their wives were unfaithful and they unknowingly then had relations

[14] Ibid., chap. 3.

[15] Ibid., chap. 8.

[16] Ibid., chap. 5.

[17] Ibid., chap. 4.

[18] Felix Just, S.J., "Jewish Groups at the Time of Jesus," Catholic-Resources.org, October 19, 2001, https://catholic-resources.org/Bible/Jewish_Groups.htm#Essenes.

with them.[19] However, celibacy was also seen as a way to anticipate the coming Messiah(s). Celibacy would have been common especially for those not married but, even in the case of married couples, they would voluntarily abstain from marital relations for up to three years in order to subdue sexual appetites while still observing God's command to be fruitful and multiply.[20]

Brant Pitre also points out in *Jesus and the Jewish Roots of Mary* that there is a biblical basis, particularly in the Book of Numbers, for evidence of vows of virginity that could be taken by Jewish women:

> If she is married to a husband, while under her vows or any thoughtless utterance of her lips by which she has bound herself, and her husband hears of it, and says nothing to her on the day that he hears; then her vows shall stand, and her pledges by which she has bound herself shall stand. But if, on the day that her husband comes to hear of it, he expresses disapproval, then he shall make void her vow which was on her, and the thoughtless utterance of her lips, by which she bound herself; and the Lord will forgive her.... Any vow and any binding oath to afflict herself, her husband may establish, or her husband may make void. But if her husband says nothing to her from day to day, then he establishes all her vows, or all her pledges, that are upon her; he has established them, because he said nothing

[19] Lawrence H. Shiffman, *Reclaiming the Dead Sea Scrolls : The History of Judaism, the Background of Christianity, the Lost Library of Qumran* (Jewish Publication Society, 1994), 127–128.

[20] Josephus, *Of the War*, bk. 2, *Penelope*, University of Chicago, accessed August 22, 2024, chap. 8, sec. 13, https://penelope.uchicago.edu/josephus/war-2.html.

> to her on the day that he heard of them. But if he makes them null and void after he has heard of them, then he shall bear her iniquity. These are the statutes which the Lord commanded Moses, as between a man and his wife. (30:6–8, 13–16, RSVCE)

To "afflict herself," in this context, could refer to fasting but would also include abstinence from sexual relations.[21] We can also see that, similar to a Nazirite vow, husbands and fathers would have the ability to nullify such a vow of virginity; importantly, Numbers indicates that if a woman's vow is accepted by her husband, her vow becomes perpetual.[22] A vow such as this would likely have been for spiritual reasons and would be the most similar precursor to consecrated life that can be seen in the Scriptures.

Virginity and Symbolism in the Old Testament

Virginity itself plays into the most frequent symbology present in Scripture, which is that of marriage or bride and groom. Israel, God's Chosen People, is frequently referred to as "virgin Israel" or "virgin daughter," and there are many instances in the writings of the prophets (and others) that speak of Israel as virgin (Ps. 45:14, Isa. 62:5, Jer. 31:4, Jer. 46:11, to name a few). Here, the sense is not one of physical intactness, because it is a spiritual betrothal that has happened between God and His people, but a reality of fidelity.

Virginity is seen to be related to wholeness and to faithfulness. Israel is asked to observe the *Shema*, which was recited morning and evening:

21 Brant Pitre, *Jesus and the Jewish Roots of Mary: Unveiling the Mother of the Messiah* (Image Publishing, 2018), 97.

22 Ibid., 98.

> Cover your eyes with your right hand and say: Hear, O Israel, the L-rd is our G-d, the L-rd is One. Recite the following verse in an undertone: Blessed be the name of the glory of His kingdom forever and ever. Blessed be the name of the glory of His kingdom forever and ever. You shall love the L-rd your G-d with all your heart, with all your soul, and with all your might. And these words which I command you today shall be upon your heart. You shall teach them thoroughly to your children, and you shall speak of them when you sit in your house and when you walk on the road, when you lie down and when you rise. You shall bind them as a sign upon your hand, and they shall be for a reminder between your eyes. And you shall write them upon the doorposts of your house and upon your gates.[23]

The call to observe the Shema means that the whole person needs to be given to God, who has made a covenant with the people. Heart, soul, and might together symbolize the totality of all the faculties and facets of the person, and all of it belongs to God alone. The people were to love God with all their being, and we can see, over and over again, the pattern of alternating idolatry and faithfulness with respect to Israel's relationship with God, which is frequently referred to in the contrasting terms *adultery* or *prostitution* and *virginity*, respectively.

Though virginity in the Scriptures is not given a reductive understanding of physical intactness, it doesn't mean that tangible

[23] "Text of the Shema Prayer in Hebrew and English," Chabad.org, published by Kehot Publication Society, accessed July 7, 2024, https://www.chabad.org/library/article_cdo/aid/706163/jewish/Text-of-the-Shema-Prayer-in-Hebrew-and-English.htm#lt=primary.

signs of the faithfulness virginity signaled were not present in the culture. Israel was asked to use many external signs as a means of recalling this marriage covenant between God and His people, including circumcision, use of tefillin (two black boxes worn on the forearm and forehead, each containing Scripture passages), prayer shawls, and more.[24] Blessings also form part of the external signs. I remember having coffee with a Jewish rabbi whom I had occasion to work with, and she described some of the many blessings; for example, when seeing a person you hadn't seen in a long time (a blessing that was akin to thanking God for someone returning from the dead!) or before sending a family member on a trip.

It's very important to note that the responsibility for virginal intactness, both in terms of women prior to marriage and in terms of the faithfulness of the people, was not just one-sided on the part of Israel. God's providential and tender care is also evident throughout Scriptures and far eclipses the completeness with which Israel could cling to God in faithfulness. There are beautiful images in Song of Songs and throughout the Old Testament of the protectiveness of God for His people—for virgin Israel—and of the descriptive care that the people of Israel, and the fathers in particular, were to exercise in the care of their virgin daughters. These are the fundamental understandings of virginity, in addition to the absence of sexual activity, that come from Judaism: wholeness, faithfulness, betrothal as an "already" of marriage. These principles were present in the context of a culture where virginity and marriage were both prized highly at their appropriate times.

24 "Tefillin (Phylacteries)," My Jewish Learning, accessed August 22, 2024, https://www.myjewishlearning.com/article/tefillin-phylacteries/.

Virginity in the First Centuries of the Church

The presence of Nazirites, the community of the Essenes, and the likelihood of vows of virginity among some Jewish women reveal that celibacy, though for varying reasons, was not entirely unknown at the time of Christ:

> Certainly that tradition was connected in some way with Israel's expectation of the Messiah's coming, especially among the women of Israel from whom he was to be born. In fact, the ideal of celibacy and virginity for the sake of greater closeness to God was not entirely foreign to certain Jewish circles, especially in the period immediately preceding the coming of Jesus. Nevertheless, celibacy for the sake of the Kingdom, or rather virginity, is undeniably an innovation connected with the incarnation of God.[25]

In Acts 18:18, Luke writes that Paul "had his hair cut off at Cenchreae because of a vow he had taken." In Acts 21:23–24 we read: "So do what we tell you. There are four men with us who have made a vow. Take these men, join in their purification rites and pay their expenses, so that they can have their heads shaved." This and other evidence suggest that it was likely that early Christians took a Nazirite vow, and that St. Paul himself may have been one of them, and also possibly James the Apostle. Almost certainly, John the Baptist was under a lifelong Nazirite vow.

There are many biblical references to virginity in the New Testament. These include the first instance in Matthew 19:12,

[25] John Paul II, apostolic letter *Mulieris dignitatem* (On the Dignity and Vocation of Women) (August 15, 1988), no. 20, https://www.vatican.va/content/john-paul-ii/en/apost_letters/1988/documents/hf_jp-ii_apl_19880815_mulieris-dignitatem.html.

where Christ speaks of those who are eunuchs "for the sake of the Kingdom" of God, with an indication that this gift of celibacy is not given to all. Tradition has always taken this to mean that a vow of perpetual continence can be taken by those whom the Lord calls, and that this is directed toward extending the kingdom of God.

St. Paul, in 1 Corinthians 7:25–40, speaks of the good of marriage, but also of the preference for those to stay "as he is," and he gives a number of reasons for this, which we will also look more at later, but which are focused on the freedom of one who is celibate to be able to devote oneself to the things of God. It is for this reason that "the Church, following this teaching of St. Paul, has always considered the state of virginity or celibacy preferable in itself to the state of marriage, and the Council of Trent (Sess. XXIV, Can. 10) pronounces an anathema against the opposite doctrine."[26] This has sometimes been used to diminish marriage as something inferior to consecrated life, but Fr. Raniero Cantalamessa gives a helpful lens when he says, "I believe that is not ontologically (that is, in itself) a more perfect state, but it is an eschatologically more advanced state, in the sense that it is more like the definitive state towards which we are all journeying."[27] The time of the Council of Trent was also on the heels of the Protestant Reformation, and responded to many of the challenges brought by Martin Luther and others, one of which was a challenge to the validity and goodness of celibacy for the sake of the kingdom.

[26] Arthur Vermeersch, "Virginity," New Advent, accessed September 25, 2022, http://www.newadvent.org/cathen/15458a.htm.

[27] Raniero Cantalamessa, *Virginity: A Positive Approach to Celibacy for the Sake of the Kingdom*, trans. Charles Serignat (St. Paul's Publishing, 1995), 7.

Moving forward, in his tracing of the history of consecrated virginity, René Metz says:

> Interestingly, in the ritual for consecration of virgins in the 9th and 10th centuries, there is a "Blessing of St. Matthew" that reflects an ancient oral tradition found in the 'Passion of St. Matthew' dating back to the 6th century. According to the 'Passion of St. Matthew,' the apostle evangelized Ethiopia and converted King Egypus along with his whole court to the Christian faith. After the death of King Egypus, his successor to the throne, Hyratacus, wanted to marry his daughter Iphigenie and beseeched St. Matthew to intercede on his behalf. According to the legend, Iphigenie would not hear of marriage to Hyratacus since she had already promised her life to Christ. She begged St. Matthew to consecrate her and several companions as virgins, which he did most readily. He imposed hands on her and prayed a prayer of consecration, 'Deus plamator corporum' which asked God to preserve her from carnal desires and to give her the desire for heavenly things. This action resulted in St. Matthew's martyrdom.[28]

Spontaneous Development of a Virginal Charism

The writings of the early Church Fathers are the main source for Church Tradition regarding consecrated virginity. *Ecclesiae Sponsae Imago* lists a number of them:

- Clement of Rome (35–99): "Let him that is pure in the flesh not grow proud of it, and boast, knowing that it was

[28] René Metz, "La Consécration des Vierges dans l'Église Romaine," *Revue d'histoire de l'Église de France* 41 (1955): 205–206.

another who bestowed on him the gift of continence."[29] There are other writings on virginity attributed to Clement, but there is significant doubt about their authenticity.

- St. Polycarp (69–155): refers to the "ordo Virginum" as well as orders of deacons and widows.[30]
- St. Justin Martyr (100–165): "And many, both men and women, who have been Christ's disciples from childhood, remain pure at the age of sixty or seventy years; and I boast that I could produce such from every race of men." [31]
- Athenagoras of Athens (133–190): "You would find many among us, both men and women, growing old unmarried, in hope of living in closer communion with God."[32]

The writings of the Fathers generally focus on those who are remaining in an unmarried state to give themselves completely to God. There is a large focus on virginity as the means by which the woman, wholly intact in body and soul, can make a gift of herself in response to God's invitation and the recognition of the bishop. *Ecclesiae Sponsae Imago* also states that, "In the Apostolic Constitutions of the second half of the fourth century, virgins appear together with widows and deaconesses, as an institutional component of the Christian community."[33]

29 Clement of Rome, *Epistle to the Corinthians*, chap. 28, New Advent, accessed July 10, 2024, https://www.newadvent.org/fathers/1010.htm.

30 *Epistle of Polycarp to the Philippians*, chap. 5, New Advent, accessed July 10, 2024, https://www.newadvent.org/fathers/0136.htm.

31 Justin Martyr, *First Apology*, no. 15, New Advent, accessed July 10, 2024, https://www.newadvent.org/fathers/0126.htm.

32 Athenagoras of Athens, *A Plea for the Christians*, chap. 33, New Advent, accessed July 10, 2024, https://www.newadvent.org/fathers/0205.htm.

33 *Ecclesiae Sponsae Imago*, 29n4.

It should also be noted that, although some have accused the Fathers of Manichaeism (which holds that sexuality is bad or intrinsically impure) or Gnosticism (seeing the physical as evil and the spiritual as good), many of their writings on continence for the kingdom or virginity are accompanied by, or sometimes interspersed with, writings that speak of the goodness of marriage and procreation and the holiness of both. For example, John of Damascus writes, "Virginity is the rule of life among the angels, the property of all incorporeal nature. This we say without speaking ill of marriage: God forbid! (for we know that the Lord blessed marriage by His presence . . .)."[34] Another example comes from St. Ambrose: "We are taught that the virtue of chastity is threefold, one kind that of married life, a second that of widowhood, and the third that of virginity, for we do not so set forth one as to exclude others. . . . The training of the Church is rich in this, that it has those whom it may set before others, but has none whom it rejects."[35]

The Witness of the Virgin Martyrs

There are many virgin martyrs included in the martyrology, including Agatha of Catania, Lucy of Syracuse, Agnes and Cecilia of Rome, Thecla of Iconium, Apollonia of Alexandria, Restituta of Carthage, and Justa and Rufina of Seville.[36] The Fathers saw in the deaths of these women the culmination and most clear image of the total dedication to Christ that was recognized by the early

[34] John of Damascus, *An Exposition of the Orthodox Faith*, bk. 4, chap. 24, accessed July 10, 2024, https://www.newadvent.org/fathers/3304.htm.

[35] Ambrose, *Concerning Widows*, chap. 4, no. 23, New Advent, accessed July 10, 2024, https://www.newadvent.org/fathers/3408.htm.

[36] *Ecclesiae Sponsae Imago*, no. 2.

Church. Further (and more explicit) writings of the Church Fathers on consecrated virginity show they referred to consecrated virgins as *Sponsae Christi* (brides of Christ), *Christo dedicate* (dedicated to Christ), *Christo maritatae* (married to Christ), and *Deo nuptiae* (brides of God).[37]

Cyprian wrote one of the first treatises specifically on consecrated virgins called *De habitu virginum* (on the dress of virgins), which is less about what to wear and more about the virtue of chastity in those who have consecrated their lives to Christ in a special way. Sr. Angela Elizabeth Keenan writes:

> Before Cyprian's time we know simply of the existence of groups of Christians who aimed to lead a more perfect life; beyond this our knowledge is extremely limited. Clement of Alexandria [*in Quis dives salvetur* 36] notes that in addition to the faithful there are the "elect of the elect who draw themselves, like ships to the strand, out of the surge of the world to a place of safety"— those whom the "Word calls the 'light of the world' and the 'salt of the earth.'" Origen [in *In numer* II homily, N1], in his enumeration of dignitaries, mentions first the bishop, the priest, the deacon, and the sacerdotal orders, and from these passes to the virgins and the continent. Hippolytus [in *Fragments in proverbial* PL 10.627] introduces the ascetics in an enumeration of the seven divine orders which sustain the society of the faithful, thus ranking them as a distinct body among the prophets, martyrs, priests, saints, and the just.[38]

37 Ibid.

38 Cyprian, "De Habitu Virginum," in *The Fathers of the Church: St Cyprian Treatises*, trans. Sr. Angela Elizabeth Keenan, SND (Catholic University of America Press, 1958), 25–26.

What the earliest letters show us is that there was a vow that was likely private at first, and that the vow did not include surrendering of property or any kind of vow of poverty, nor is there any kind of positive indication of any kind of community life at that point that would resemble what we now see as religious life.[39] Cyprian writes,

> You say that you are wealthy and rich, and you think that you should use those things which God has willed you to possess. Use them, certainly, but for the things of salvation; use them, but for good purposes; use them, but for those things which God has commanded, and which the Lord has set forth. Let the poor feel that you are wealthy; let the needy feel that you are rich. Lend your estate to God; give food to Christ.[40]

De Habitu Virginum also indicates that there was a proliferation of women living in this way:

> This is the flower of the ecclesiastical seed, the grace and ornament of spiritual endowment, a joyous disposition, the wholesome and uncorrupted work of praise and honour, God's image answering to the holiness of the Lord, the more illustrious portion of Christ's flock. The glorious fruitfulness of Mother Church rejoices by their means, and in them abundantly flourishes; and in proportion as a copious virginity is added to her number, so much the more it increases the joy of the Mother.[41]

[39] Ibid., 2.

[40] Cyprian, *On the Dress of Virgins*, 11, EWTN, accessed July 10, 2024, https://www.ewtn.com/catholicism/library/on-the-dress-of-virgins-de-habitu-virginum-11407.

[41] Ibid., 3.

The writings of the Fathers do not indicate that virgins were primarily *doing* things but were rather living the Christian life more perfectly (in the aforementioned understanding of the term "perfect"), and thereby making the everlasting kingdom of the Father present in the world now, simply through their existence. Partly, this is because the early Church expected the return of Christ to be immanent, and many were expecting it to occur within their lifetime. Cyprian writes to the virgins, "That which we shall be, you have already begun to be. You possess already in this world the glory of the resurrection. You pass through the world without the contagion of the world; in that you continue chaste and virgins, you are equal to the angels of God."[42] Gregory of Nyssa writes:

> If, then, death cannot pass beyond virginity, but finds his power checked and shattered there, it is demonstrated that virginity is a stronger thing than death; and that body is rightly named undying which does not lend its service to a dying world, nor brook to become the instrument of a succession of dying creatures.[43]

Along these lines, there are also writings pertaining to virgins who were not living according to this ideal. Cyprian writes:

> For this reason, therefore, the Church frequently mourns over her virgins; hence she groans at their scandalous and detestable stories; hence the flower of her virgins is extinguished, the honour and modesty of continency are injured, and all its glory and dignity are profaned. Thus

42 Ibid., 22.

43 Gregory of Nyssa, *On Virginity*, chap. 13, New Advent, accessed July 10, 2024, https://www.newadvent.org/fathers/2907.htm.

> the hostile besieger insinuates himself by his arts; thus by snares that deceive, by secret ways, the devil creeps in. Thus, while virgins wish to be more carefully adorned, and to wander with more liberty, they cease to be virgins, corrupted by a furtive dishonour; widows before they are married, adulterous, not to their husband, but to Christ. In proportion as they had been as virgins destined to great rewards, so will they experience great punishments for the loss of their virginity.[44]

Virgins were seen in their way of life to be following closely to the virgin Christ. Augustine of Hippo writes, "But, lo, That Lamb goes by a Virgin road, how shall they go after Him, who have lost what there is no way for them to recover? Do ye, therefore, do ye go after Him, His virgins; do ye there also go after Him, in that on this one account wherever He shall have gone."[45] Gregory of Nyssa also affirmed in his writings that virginity is a charism and a grace that not all are called to.[46]

Development of a Liturgical Rite and Ordo

There is solid evidence of a Rite of Consecration from the fourth century on, which was presided over by the diocesan bishop with the community gathered for Mass, and during which the woman gave her *sanctum propositum* to remain a virgin forever followed by the bishop's pronouncement of the prayer of consecration.[47] "In

44 Cyprian, *On the Dress of Virgins*, 20.

45 Augustine, *Of Holy Virginity*, 29, New Advent, accessed July 10, 2024, https://www.newadvent.org/fathers/1310.htm.

46 Gregory of Nyssa, *On Virginity*, chap. 1.

47 *Ecclesiae Sponsae Imago*, no. 3.

the Rite, those to be consecrated express the *sanctum propositum* (the holy resolution). This is the firm and definitive resolve to persevere for their whole life in perfect chastity, and in the service of God and the Church, following Christ in accordance with the Gospel, to give the world a living witness of love and to be a clear sign of the future Kingdom."[48] Further, "As affirmed already in the writings of Ambrose of Milan and subsequently, starting from the most ancient liturgical sources, the nuptial symbolism of the rite was displayed particularly by the bestowal of the veil on the virgin by the bishop, a gesture that corresponded to the *velatio* (placing of the marriage veil) that took place during the marriage celebration."[49]

Some elements in the writings of the Fathers start to become increasingly clear in terms of their details, such as the reservation of the act of consecration to the bishop, and the age a woman could receive the consecration (twelve at first and then moved to sixteen up to age sixty, which was the entry age for the Order of Widows). The virgins came to be known as a distinct order of women, which is a different use of the word "order" than is used in the term "religious order"; it simply refers to the total body of all women who have received the consecration as opposed to distinct bodies of men and women who make up a religious community. Here is a quote from St. Basil that illustrates many of the characteristics in one place that we have seen so far scattered in other Fathers' writings, along with some of the concerns of bishops for women who were not faithful to their *propositum* (their holy resolution to remain perpetual virgins):

[48] Ibid., no. 19.

[49] Ibid., no. 3.

Concerning fallen virgins, who, after professing a chaste life before the Lord, make their vows vain, because they have fallen under the lusts of the flesh, our fathers, tenderly and meekly making allowance for the infirmities of them that fall, laid down that they might be received after a year, ranking them with the digamists [one who is marrying a second time]. Since, however, by God's grace the Church grows mightier as she advances, and the order of virgins is becoming more numerous, it is my judgment that careful heed should be given both to the act as it appears upon consideration, and to the mind of Scripture, which may be discovered from the context. Widowhood is inferior to virginity; consequently the sin of the widows comes far behind that of the virgins.... If, therefore, a widow lies under a very heavy charge, as setting at naught her faith in Christ, what must we think of the virgin, who is the bride of Christ, and a chosen vessel dedicated to the Lord?... The name *virgin* is given to a woman who voluntarily devotes herself to the Lord, renounces marriage, and embraces a life of holiness. And we admit professions dating from the age of full intelligence. For it is not right in such cases to admit the words of mere children. But a girl of sixteen or seventeen years of age, in full possession of her faculties, who has been submitted to strict examination, and is then constant, and persists in her entreaty to be admitted, may then be ranked among the virgins, her profession ratified, and its violation rigorously punished. Many girls are brought forward by their parents and brothers, and other kinsfolk, before they are of full age, and have no inner impulse towards a celibate life.... Such women as these must not be readily received, before we have made public investigation of their own sentiments.[50]

Gradual Decline and Subsequent Resurgence of the Order of Virgins

Consecrated virgins generally lived with their own families. However, "as cenobitic monasticism developed the Church associated virginal consecration with community life, and therefore with the observance of a common rule and obedience to a superior. Over the course of centuries, the original way of life of the *Ordo virginum*, with its characteristic foundations in the local ecclesial community under the guidance of the diocesan bishop, gradually disappeared."[51] As monastic orders grew up, there were two distinct groups of consecrated virgins: those in monasteries and those continuing to live in the world.[52] Increasingly, consecrated virgins tended toward monastic communities and, around the ninth to tenth centuries, were rarely found living in the world. Some Carmelite orders retained the consecration of virgins as a rite that some women received prior to solemn vows, and there were also some mendicant orders where the rite was adapted and incorporated into the ceremonies for the profession of vows, but the consecration was no longer received by women living outside of this context.

50 Basil, *Letter 199 to Amphilochius*, no. 18, New Advent, accessed July 10, 2024, https://www.newadvent.org/fathers/3202199.htm.

51 *Ecclesiae Sponsae Imago*, no. 5.

52 Mary Kay Lacke, "Historical Overview of the Vocation of Consecrated Virgin in the Catholic Church," in *An Introduction to the Vocation of Consecrated Virginity Lived in the World*, vol. 1 (United States Association of Consecrated Virgins, 2012), 88.

In 1139, the Second Lateran Council suppressed the Rite of Consecration of a Virgin Living in the World. However, in 1924, Anne Leflaive (1899–1987) received the consecration of a virgin under the hands of her bishop, Hyacinthe-Jean Chassagnon of Autun following the encouragement of François de Rovérié de Cabrières of Montpellier. Following this, there was an increase in requests to receive the consecration, and the Congregation for Institutes of Consecrated Life was asked for clarification. In 1927, they replied in the negative and argued that the consecration of virgins living in the world had long ago fallen into disuse and would be in contradiction for present canon laws. They suggested that women take a private vow of virginity if necessary, but were also concerned that receiving a public consecration could give those receiving it a sense of false superiority or possibly deter women from vocations to religious life.

Over the following decades, Anne Leflaive petitioned the Vatican continually to reinstate the consecration, and even met with Angelo Roncalli (the future Pope John XXIII) and Giovanni Montini (the future Pope Paul VI) to make her requests known. Both were receptive to her ideas. In 1963, the Second Vatican Council requested a revision of the Rite of the Consecration of Virgins that was found in the Roman Pontifical. The revised rite was approved by Pope Paul VI and published on May 31, 1970. This consecration could be bestowed either on women in monastic orders or on women living in the world, the form of life that had been found in the early Church. Elizabeth Bailey was the first woman consecrated under the revised rite in 1972 in England—the first in England since the third century.

John Paul II wrote this in reference to the *Ordo Virginum:*

> It is a source of joy and hope to witness in our time a new flowering of *the ancient Order of Virgins*, known in Christian

> communities ever since apostolic times. Consecrated by the diocesan bishop, these women acquire a particular link with the Church, which they are committed to serve while remaining in the world. Either alone or in association with others, they constitute *a special eschatological image of the Heavenly Bride and of the life to come*, when the Church will at last fully live her love for Christ the Bridegroom.[53]

Since the 1970 promulgation, Canon Law was updated in 1983 to reflect the norms of consecrated virginity. In 1995 there was the first gathering of the *Ordo Virginum* in Rome, with Pope St. John Paul II present. In 2004 the Directory for the Pastoral Ministry of Bishops included information regarding the *Ordo Virginum*, and there have since been a number of international gatherings in Rome, as well as the publication of *Ecclesiae Sponsae Imago* in 2018.

Practical Applications: The Order of Virgins Today

There are now approximately five thousand consecrated virgins in the world with varying receptions to consecrated virginity, country to country and diocese to diocese. In some places where there is a desire to welcome consecrated virginity vocations, there are still questions and challenges remaining with respect to adequate formation for women. Some dioceses with smaller or remote populations also face considerable obstacles in terms of accompaniment of women in formation and in providing communal opportunities with other consecrated women, which is necessary

[53] John Paul II, post-synodal apostolic exhortation *Vita consecrata* (On the Consecrated Life) (March 25, 1996), no. 7, https://www.vatican.va/content/john-paul-ii/en/apost_exhortations/documents/hf_jp-ii_exh_25031996_vita-consecrata.html.

for those in consecrated life, though it's helpful to note that a growing body of organizations and resources are springing up to assist bishops and women in these circumstances. Currently, bishops across the world have largely welcomed inquiries regarding consecrated virgins and have been working collaboratively to establish prudent and helpful formation programs for women who are called to this vocation.

However, this means that there are still many "on the ground" questions about everything from formation approach to how and where the consecration Mass is celebrated to how bishops relate to consecrated virgins in their diocese. Many women who received the consecration prior to the publication of *Ecclesiae Sponsae Imago* had a longer or shorter formation process than the document recommends, and their formation may or may not have included theological study or formation regarding the nature and living of consecrated virginity. In this sense, many dioceses in the Church may have to play a bit of "catch up" with women who are already consecrated. It's not necessarily a matter of putting women through a formation program now, but it *is* certainly a matter of ensuring that those who are consecrated virgins, a public vocation in the Church, understand their own vocation adequately and can communicate its fundamental meanings to those they encounter.

Further, regarding those who are currently in formation, or who will be formed in the coming years, there are no set programs that must be followed, though there are general guidelines. This is intentional to some degree, because the Holy See respects both the widely disparate resources and realities among dioceses, as well as the authority of the diocesan bishop to discern how formation and support for the *Ordo Virginum* will take place. However, practically speaking, this means that bishops are left with a significant task of creating formation programs either from scratch or with materials or recommendations from other bishops or formators. Again, this is, to some degree, very necessary because the reality of each woman and each diocese is unique, but at the same time it presents some challenges because a lack of a certain commonality in formation elements may lead to widely disparate experiences of consecrated virgins across the globe. There are, potentially, significantly harmful consequences that may damage the force of the public witness of the vocation if, for example, women are not adequately formed in their capacity to live an integrated celibate sexuality. However, it should also be noted that several countries have national associations of consecrated virgins that have produced resources or put together recommendations for formation. With the increase in women receiving the consecration, bishops are also increasingly relying on those consecrated virgins with theological or other appropriate training to provide formation that is tailored to consecrated virginity.

It's likely we will see further and more detailed documents from the Holy See (or even from national bishops' conferences) relating to many aspects of consecrated virginity, and that bishops will continue to confer with each other as they discern their own approaches to supporting consecrated virginity within their respective dioceses. However, as these things remain forthcoming, some amount of responsibility has fallen to women who feel called to this vocation—especially in places where the *Ordo Virginum* is not already established.

I have personally spoken with several women who are the first of their diocese to begin formation for consecrated virginity. Some are working with very proactive bishops who have personally invited women of the diocese to come forward if they sense they may be called to consecrated virginity, but most have, after approaching their bishop and finding that he is open to having consecrated virgins in the diocese, taken some measure of responsibility for assisting him with the preparation of a formation program, or at least with spurring on the process. It may not be the case in other countries, but at least in Canada, many bishops have reached out to their brother bishops who already have the *Ordo* established in their dioceses, which is very encouraging. Remarkably, many, many of the women who have received the consecration in Canada in the last several years have come into formation with prior theological study or significant experiences, such as prior time spent in a religious order. Further, there is already an excellent networking that is happening between women who have received the consecration (as well as those currently in formation), and these relationships are helping to support bishops and others tasked with initial and ongoing formation of consecrated virgins. It seems as though the Lord, who appears to be calling an increasing number of women in Canada, is providing a very solid ground for this to happen.

All this to say, if you are a woman who is discerning consecrated virginity, you may encounter a vastly different reality than a woman from another diocese. If there are not other consecrated virgins in your diocese already, or even if there are but formation programs are still in their initial years, you may find that you are part of the challenging and exciting path around a vocation that is new, even if it is ancient. Regardless, when the Lord calls, the particular challenges of your journey are not unknown to Him, and He will use them—both for your good and the good of those who will come after you.

Questions and Scriptures for Reflection

1. What strikes me most in this chapter? What virgin Saints would I like to know more about?

2. Where do I see room to grow in our current understanding of this vocation and how to live it?

3. Thinking of Anne Leflaive, how might I help this vocation to be known and loved?

Judges 11
Psalm 45
Isaiah 43:16-21
Isaiah 62
Hebrews 10:23
1 Thessalonians 5:23-24

3

Ecclesiology and Diocesan Character

To be in dialogue with God implies being open to all creatures. Dialogue with God is linked to the Body of Christ. Therefore, Christian virginity always has an ecclesial character. With her yes at the Annunciation, Mary became the first Church, because the Church, in her most fundamental nature, is no other than the yes of the creature to God.[54]

Love the Church: she is your mother. Through the solemn rite presided over by the diocesan Bishop (Ordo consecrationis virginum; *Praenotanda, n. 6, p. 8), you have received from her the gift of consecration; you have been dedicated to her service. You must always feel closely bound to the Church.*[55]

[54] Joseph Cardinal Ratzinger, "Gift in the Church and for the Church," homily for the Mass of Consecration of a Virgin (March 25, 1988), https://diolc.org/wp-content/uploads/2019/05/50th-Anniversary_Material_rev_02JULY19.pdf.

[55] John Paul II, "May Christ Be Your Total and Exclusive Love," address to consecrated virgins (June 14, 1995), no. 5, https://diolc.org/files/consecratedlife/Pope%20John%20Paul%20II%201995%20Presentation.pdf.

Where Does Consecrated Virginity Fit Among Other Vocations?

When speaking of vocations, most people are familiar with the major three: marriage, priesthood, and consecrated life (though many think consecrated life consists of religious life alone). It's necessary to unfold these three areas to find a more comprehensive view of vocations, especially with respect to helping people understand what consecrated virginity is and how it fits in among the other vocations. It's helpful to visualize the various vocations in the Church as branches belonging to a tree, similar to the one pictured here (inspired by The Vocations Tree used by the United States Association of Consecrated Virgins).[56]

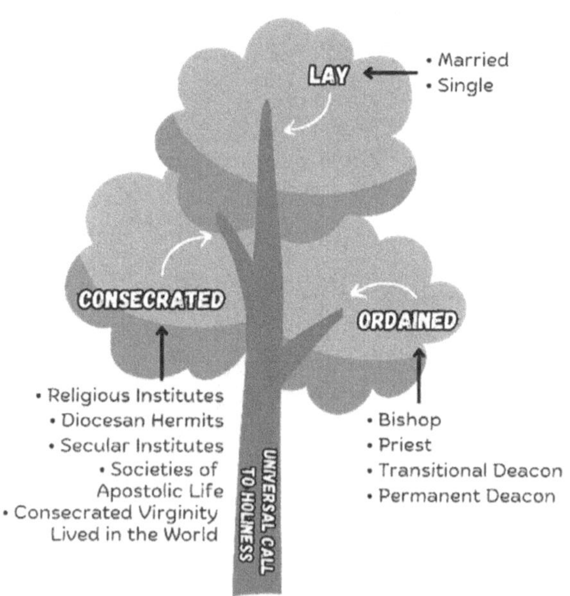

[56] United States Association of Consecrated Virgins and Jennifer Ward, "The Vocation Tree," USACV, accessed August 3, 2024, https://www.vocationtree.org/vocation-tree.

Foundationally, trees require the sustenance provided to their roots by soil and water, and this is an image of the waters of Baptism and the sacraments of the Church that provide the grace of God that nourishes all vocations. From its roots, the Church grows up out of our baptismal call and sacramental life, and the trunk of the tree represents our most fundamental vocation, which is the call to holiness:

> The Lord Jesus, the divine Teacher and Model of all perfection, preached holiness of life to each and everyone of His disciples of every condition. He Himself stands as the author and consumator of this holiness of life: "Be you therefore perfect, even as your heavenly Father is perfect". Indeed He sent the Holy Spirit upon all men that He might move them inwardly to love God with their whole heart and their whole soul, with all their mind and all their strength and that they might love each other as Christ loves them. The followers of Christ are called by God, not because of their works, but according to His own purpose and grace. They are justified in the Lord Jesus, because in the baptism of faith they truly become sons of God and sharers in the divine nature. In this way they are really made holy. Then too, by God's gift, they must hold on to and complete in their lives this holiness they have received.[57]

Every Christian is called to be holy, first and foremost. This means that no one is shut out of a vocation, because all of us have

[57] Vatican Council II, Dogmatic Constitution *Lumen gentium* (Light of Nations) (November 21, 1964), no. 40, https://www.vatican.va/archive/hist_councils/ii_vatican_council/documents/vat-ii_const_19641121_lumen-gentium_en.html.

the vocation to be "sharers in the divine nature." However, there are more specific vocations through which people serve God and their fellow men in a particular way and experience an intensification of their own sanctification. This is what is represented by the three large tree branches.

These three larger branches represent the three states in life: lay (people called to bring the Gospel into all the world), ordained (the teaching, governing and sanctifying ministry of the bishop which extends through ordination to presbyters and deacons), and consecrated (those called to live directly or in an adapted way as Christ Himself, who was poor, chaste and obedient, and to reveal and incarnate the coming kingdom).[58] There are multiple layers to this in real life, because people can be both deacons and husbands, for example, or men can be ordained but also be members of a religious order.

The largest of these branches is the marriage one, because most people are called to marriage. Within this lay branch, though, are included those who are single. The question of whether and how the single life is a vocation in the Church is something that there are divergent opinions on. Some dioceses list singleness as a vocation on their websites, some cultures have specific words to describe such a vocation ("Blessed Singleness" in the Philippines, for example), and others, including vocations directors, bishops and theologians, are hesitant to speak of a vocation to single life, or deny it is possible at all.

[58] John Paul II, post-synodal apostolic exhortation *Christifideles laici* (Lay Members of Christ's Faithful People) (December 30, 1988), no. 15, https://www.vatican.va/content/john-paul-ii/en/apost_exhortations/documents/hf_jp-ii_exh_30121988_christifideles-laici.html.

This question of whether and how singleness is a vocation is in desperate need of more clarity. There are certainly those who feel called by the Lord to remain single, for example, because they have LGBT experiences, or because they have a particular ministry or profession that requires an extraordinary dedication that would not be possible in the context of marriage and family life or in other forms of consecrated life. Many persons make private promises of celibacy for the sake of the kingdom, but this is different than something that is a publicly recognized vocation which comes with its own rights and responsibilities. It's also interesting to note that there is no male "version" of consecrated virginity. Canon 605 specifically leaves the door open to new forms of consecrated life, so it's possible that some of those who are now considered "dedicated singles" may inspire new ways of being consecrated fully to the service of the Lord and the Church.[59]

The next branch represents the three degrees of Holy Orders: bishop, presbyter and deacon. Deacons are either permanent—that is, ordained "unto the ministry" for assisting with some liturgical roles and for various charitable ministries—or transitional, meaning that they are ordained to the diaconate as a step toward the priesthood. Priests (the presbyterate) are co-workers with the bishop and help him to fulfill his ecclesial ministry, which is to teach, govern, and sanctify the people of God in his diocese in communion with the successor of Peter. Those who belong to this "branch" may also belong to another, such as permanent deacons who are also married, or priests who belong to a Religious Institute.

[59] *Code of Canon Law*, January 23, 1983, Can. 605, https://www.vatican.va/archive/cod-iuris-canonici/eng/documents/cic_lib2-cann573-606_en.html.

The branch representing consecrated life contains the widest number of possibilities, and includes Diocesan Hermits, Religious Institutes (either contemplative or active), Secular Institutes, Societies of Apostolic Life, and, of course, Consecrated Virginity Lived in the World. Societies of Apostolic Life are included in this branch because they fall under the governance of the same Dicastery responsible for consecrated life. However, Canon Law does state that they resemble institutes of consecrated life but are not identical to it.[60] Sometimes we also hear about Third Orders. These are a unique vocation through which a person adopts a particular spiritual heritage and way of life in accord with the character of the religious order from which it springs. Examples would be Third Order Franciscans, Dominicans, and Carmelites and Oblates of St. Benedict. It's important to know that someone who becomes an associate to an Institute as a Third Order member can do so *in addition* to entering into another vocation (with some exceptions such as Third Order Regular Franciscans who profess the evangelical counsels). So, a married person could become a Dominican Oblate, or a consecrated virgin could become a Third Order Franciscan (also called Secular Franciscans), for example.

Distinguishing Between the Forms of Consecrated Life

Before looking at characteristics of consecrated virginity, it is helpful to look at some distinguishing characteristics of other forms of consecrated life. Diocesan hermits make vows of poverty, chastity, and obedience at the hands of their diocesan bishop, who becomes their superior. Their way of life is characterized by a strict withdrawal from

[60] *Code of Canon Law*, Can. 731.

the world to give themselves to a life of intense prayer and sacrifice which is offered for the needs of the diocese in which they reside. This is a rare vocation currently. It is, in some ways, prefigured by anchorites and anchoresses who lived mainly in the Middle Ages. Instead of residing in their own home, anchorites and anchoresses would live in a residence that was built immediately adjacent to a church, with a window or opening into the church so that they could attend Mass and receive the Eucharist. Those in the community would be responsible for bringing an anchorite or anchoress food and other necessities and would also take away waste. Anchorites and anchoresses would often enter the enclosure and the final wall of the dwelling would be built to seal them inside—meaning there was no door into or out of the enclosure—to symbolize their death to the world and entry into union with Christ. There was a rite of consecration during this process that closely resembled the funeral rite. Anchorites and anchoresses would sometimes use the windows through which necessities of life would pass to speak with people in the community and offer counsel and prayers. Though there were not many anchorites and anchoresses after the Middle Ages, one of the last notable anchoresses was Nazarena of Jesus who lived attached to a church in Rome and died in 1990.[61]

Religious institutes can be contemplative or active (though some refer to themselves as contemplative-active to indicate the primacy of a life of prayer that gives life to the apostolic works undertaken). These forms of consecrated life involve the profession of the evangelical counsels of poverty, chastity, and obedience. Religious institutes arise under the inspiration of the Holy Spirit

[61] Chris Nickson, "The Life of an Anchoress," *The History Press*, last updated July 21, 2020, https://thehistorypress.co.uk/article/the-life-of-an-anchoress/.

through a founder(s) or foundress(es) in response to some need in the Church and the world: this is referred to as the community's charism. Members of religious institutes often wear a habit or other identifiable symbols, live in community, and operate according to the constitutions of the institute.

Contemplative institutes are characterized by a strict withdrawal from the world, similar to (or even more intense than) diocesan hermits, to devote themselves to prayer and the sanctification of themselves and the world. They generally live in an enclosed monastery or convent, where either specific community members or members of the external community are responsible for things like shopping and liaising with the outside world. Most of the day (and night!) is spent in silence. Contemplative communities generally pray all the hours of the Divine Office—there are seven prescribed prayer "hours" (times) each day, though each prayer time is not a literal hour. These men and women are living in a way akin to the Desert Fathers, who would withdraw into complete solitude and practice rigorous asceticism. An example of a contemplative religious institute can be seen in the Carthusians. They live in enclosed monasteries and embrace an intensified kind of contemplative life that blends eremitic life (living in seclusion) with cenobitic life (monastic life that involves communal prayer and fellowship).

Active institutes share the same commonalities of habit, communal life, unique community charism, profession of evangelical counsels and life lived according to a community constitution. Though they are still characterized by a withdrawal from the world as those consecrated and set apart to be a sign of eternity, they generally carry out apostolates (ministries) that involve interaction with the secular world. An example of this would be the Sisters of Life who were founded in New York by Cardinal John O'Connor in 1991. Their community was founded to respond to the growing

"Culture of Death" by helping to build a "Culture of Life" through ministering to women who are vulnerable to abortion and those who have suffered the pain of abortion, and by engaging in works of life-giving evangelization. They take a fourth vow to protect and enhance the sacredness of every human life. Like some other communities, the Sisters of Life describe themselves as active-contemplative to convey the fullness of their life of prayer which informs and supports all of their apostolic activity.

Societies of apostolic life are similar to religious institutes in that their members live in common in order to observe their constitutions and carry out the charism and activities of the community received through their founder(s) or foundress(es). They also may not live the same extent of withdrawal from the secular world, depending on the vision of the founder(s) or foundress(es) and what is outlined in the community's constitutions. Unlike religious institutes, societies of apostolic life do not profess vows of poverty, chastity, and obedience. However, its members often make promises akin to the evangelical counsels, or to follow the constitutions of the community which lays out a life lived according to an adapted following of the counsels. For example, members of the Companions of the Cross, a Society of Apostolic Life based in Ottawa, Ontario, Canada, make promises to observe the community's constitutions, which lay out things like the practice of celibacy for the kingdom, how obedience is lived within the community structure, and how the community will operate financially. St. Philip Neri "can be considered the father of men's Societies of Apostolic Life."[62]

[62] "The Congregation for Institutes of Consecrated Life and Societies of Apostolic Life," Vatican.va, accessed August 2, 2024, https://www.vatican.va/roman_curia/congregations/ccscrlife/documents/rc_con_ccscrlife_profile_en.html.

Secular Institutes are relatively new in the Church in terms of their official status, as they were only recognized in Canon Law in the mid-twentieth century. However, they existed as far back as the sixteenth century.[63] Their members make vows of poverty, chastity, and obedience, but are characterized specifically by their lack of withdrawal from the world. Rather, they live in the world as a kind of leaven and share a common spirituality and way of life. They may live on their own or together.

Another vocation belonging to consecrated life that may make a comeback at some point would be the Order of Widows, whose life is similar to that of a diocesan hermit. Along with consecrated virgins, the Order of Widows is frequently mentioned in the writings of the Fathers, and there are many today who are calling for it to be revived.

Consecrated Virginity in Relation to Other Forms of Consecrated Life

So how can consecrated virginity be understood considering other consecrated vocations? Here, we can compare and contrast some elements of various forms of consecrated life in order to see the combination of elements that are unique to consecrated virginity.

We can start with the living situation. Most consecrated persons, in terms of the total population of all those living consecrated life, live in community. In fact, it is canonically necessary for most members of religious institutes and societies of apostolic life to live in community. However, diocesan hermits and some members of secular institutes are similar to consecrated virgins, in that they are not characterized by communal life. Consecrated virgins and

[63] Ibid.

those in secular institutes are not prohibited from living with other persons, and many live with family or other consecrated persons, but communal life is not intrinsic to the vocation.

The living situation of those in consecrated life is, in most cases, directly related to their relation to the secular world. Those in religious institutes, as well as diocesan hermits, are called to live with a form of withdrawal from the world. Contemplative institutes and diocesan hermits live this in the most radical way, with minimal contact with the world outside of their home or enclosure. Non-contemplative religious institutes also live in a way that fosters withdrawal from the world. Since their apostolates take place in the world, there can't be a total separation, but communities intentionally limit their participation in secular activities—such as using social media, watching television, and listening to secular music—to preserve a singular focus on Christ, communal life, and the community's mission. This separation is also supported by the visible signs used by those in religious institutes, such as the habit and the use of the titles: father, brother, sister, mother, etc.

In contrast to this, consecrated virgins and members of secular institutes are called to live their vocations "in the world" and to act as a kind of spiritual leaven. This intentional integration into the secular world is partly why consecrated virgins are not referred to as sister, and do not wear any identifiable kind of habit—refraining from these is a visible way to signify the hidden nature of the vocation. This hiddenness allows the consecrated virgin, along with the laity and members of secular institutes, access to every sphere of life in ways that the ordained and members of other forms of consecrated life do not have. It's interesting to think that, after the Second Vatican Council, many in religious institutes stopped wearing the habit with the intention of being closer to the people. While this presented a good intention at heart, it could be argued that it was an action that sterilized an aspect of the witness of religious life, and that it was errantly taking on an aspect of consecrated life not proper to it—an aspect that *is* proper to consecrated virgins.

Societies of apostolic life, though they are not characterized by the stricter withdrawal from the world seen in religious institutes, are also not characterized by the intentional integration into the world that is seen in consecrated virginity and secular institutes. Largely, the degree to which the community lives their mission "in the world" is dictated by the vision of the founder(s)/foundress(es) and the community's constitutions.

Living situations among different forms of consecrated life also reflect something important about how particular vocations are lived and what their purpose is. Most religious institutes, societies of apostolic life, and secular institutes are formed at the diocesan level and have an attachment to that diocese in the beginning stages of forming a new community. Religious institutes and societies of apostolic life also generally work closely with the bishops of dioceses they are present in and are only permitted to be in a diocese in the first place at the invitation of the diocesan bishop. However, most religious institutes and societies of apostolic life, once they have gained status as such, are governed by the Holy See through the Dicastery for Institutes of Consecrated Life and Societies of Apostolic Life. Further, most religious institutes, societies of apostolic life, and secular institutes, though most often founded in one diocese, have a presence in multiple dioceses since their charism is directed toward the universal Church, even if it is a particular population of the universal Church, such as young people or the poor.

In contrast, both diocesan hermits and consecrated virgins have a particular link to their local diocese, and both enter into their vocations at the hands of the local diocesan bishop and maintain a close relationship with him. He is, for the consecrated virgin or diocesan hermit, a spiritual father who assists them in living their vocation and relies on their prayers and support.[64] Diocesan hermits and consecrated virgins are also given their charisms by the Church primarily for the service and sanctification of the people of their particular diocese.

With respect to *who* the consecrated virgin *is*, along with women in religious institutes, she is called a Bride of Christ. The following chapters discuss this in much more detail, but from the very beginning of consecrated virginity, the Fathers referred to consecrated virgins with a variety of titles that indicated the spousal nature of her relationship with Christ. In fact, the consecrated virgin is still the only vocation in which the woman is understood to be "mystically betrothed to Christ."[65] It is from the heritage of consecrated virginity that women religious received the title "bride of Christ," and the use of nuptial or bridal imagery in vow professions and community customs varies widely between different women's religious institutes.[66] However, consecrated women, regardless of their form of consecrated life, constitute a sign of the nature of the Church, including in its Brideship to Christ, the Bridegroom: "Consecrated women are called in a very special way to *be signs of God's tender love towards the human race* and to be special witnesses to the mystery of the Church, Virgin, Bride and Mother."[67]

64 Judith Stegman, "Consecrated Virginity as a Vocation in the Catholic Church—A Vocation Tree Presentation," in *An Introduction to the Vocation of Consecrated Virginity Lived in the World*, vol. 1 (United States Association of Consecrated Virgins, 2012), 23.

65 *Code of Canon Law*, Can. 604 §1.

66 Jenna Cooper, "Who Can Be Called a Bride of Christ?," *Sponsa Christi*, last updated March 1, 2015, https://sponsa-christi.blogspot.com/2015/03/who-can-be-called-bride-of-christ.html.

67 *Vita consecrata*, no. 57.

A side note to this: despite consecrated virginity being a bridal relationship with the Lord at its most fundamental level, many people place consecrated virginity in the category of "single" vocations (assuming that singleness is a vocation in the first place). It may be that people are confused about whether singleness can somehow constitute a vocation and seeing the reality of a woman living a single life, not in community, they may automatically make conclusions about how her vocation fits into the schema of vocational life in the Church. They may even understand, by the obviousness of the name of the vocation, that the woman is living some form of consecrated life. However, in my experience there are not many people who understand that a consecrated virgin is a Bride of Christ. Considering this, it is necessary to know how to explain the vocation with some amount of succinctness, and to be able to correct people gently and affirm that we are, indeed, *not* single. We are exactly the opposite of this, like the first women in the history of the Church who were considered to be wed to the Lamb and to follow Him wherever He goes!

Finally, consecrated virginity is unique among the vocations with respect to how it is entered into. Diocesan hermits and members of religious institutes and secular institutes profess vows or promises of poverty, chastity, and obedience (as well as a fourth vow in some communities that is specific to their charism). In the case of members of societies of apostolic life, they may make promises regarding adherence to their community constitutions, or something akin to that. There is also, however, an intentional action that the person takes, as in vow professions, which, when received by the legitimate superior, incorporates them into the relevant body.

However, entry into the vocation is something passive for consecrated virgins, since they receive a consecration at the hands of the diocesan bishop. Prior to receiving it, they offer their *Sanctum*

Propositum, by which they resolve to remain a virgin for their entire lives, but this precedes the consecratory prayer and so enables but does not constitute the entry into the vocation. It is the only vocation where profession or promises are not the means by which a person is incorporated into the body of others who share in that vocation. It is conferred by the Church through the hands of the diocesan bishop and bestows a new status on the woman, that is, a bride of Christ. The woman is fundamentally changed in who she is in Christ, and she takes on all the symbolic meaning that is contained within her vocation.

There is notable bridal imagery present. In the marital embrace of a human marriage, the bride receives the bridegroom into her person, and their union is made fruitful by the intentional reception of the bride and the self-donation of the bridegroom. In the Consecration of a Virgin Living in the World, the woman receives from Christ, through the action of the diocesan bishop, the blessing by which she and Christ are mystically espoused, and through which their union becomes spiritually fruitful. This will be discussed more fully in chapter 6.

What Does It Mean for the Consecrated Virgin to Be "In the World"?

There are many elements of meaning to the phrase "in the world" that are constitutive of who the consecrated virgin is. Firstly, it is a phrase that sets her apart from other consecrated vocations and establishes clearly her call and sphere of influence. As with secular institutes, consecrated virgins in the world are *not* called to a particular withdrawal from the world. Their witness is not, as it is for members of religious institutes or hermits, to witness to singleheartedness for the Lord through the daily community horarium and the faithfulness to the community's apostolate, which is made possible by an intentional withdrawal from the normal activities that are part of life for most in the secular world.

Living "in the world" means that there is a singleheartedness for the Lord that the consecrated virgin must give priority to. The deep life of union with God that the consecrated virgin needs to cultivate is a spousal relationship that requires due care, for it is a true marriage! However, the consecrated virgin lives an embedded kind of relationship, where she is close to the majority of people, who are laypersons seeking sanctity (or whom the Lord is calling to seek sanctity, even if they do not know Him yet) in the experiences, joys, and worries of everyday life.

To live "in the world" as a consecrated virgin includes many responsibilities, such as being responsible for self-discipline and the wise use of time, ensuring one's own financial solvency, investing intentionally in friendships and community for one's own good, stewarding one's health (including mental health), prudent discernment regarding modes, times, and extents of service to others, and being solely responsible for the necessities of life in the world (even if other people help in certain areas), such as housing, bills, cooking, cleaning, employment, and so on.

There are also spiritual responsibilities, which include fulfilling the obligation to pray for the bishop, priests and people of the diocese, as well as the Holy Father, to pray the Liturgy of the Hours in union with the whole Church and for the Church, to attend to the primacy of one's spiritual life and ensure its health and growth, offering one's gifts in service to the people of the diocese (whether in faith settings or secular—all people living in the diocese are the object of the consecrated virgin's love), accepting and offering up sufferings for the people of God (in particular, for the bishop and priests), engaging in intentional penances and mortifications on behalf of the people of God, participating in the liturgical life of the diocese (including diocesan gatherings, such as ordinations and the Chrism Mass), frequenting the sacraments, and making use of devotions and sacramentals to support one's spiritual life and offer the fruits of these for those one serves. All these responsibilities are carried out "in the world"; the consecrated virgin carries out her activity in the same realm as that of the lay faithful, while carrying out the spiritual life that is common to the realm of the ordained and consecrated.

Consecrated virgins experience great freedom in a way that is arguably wider than any other vocation. Even in the case of secular institutes, where the vocation is also lived "in the world," there is a particular spirituality or way of life that governs how its members live and pray to some degree. Only in consecrated virginity is there total ability for the woman to live a unique reality that allows her to pray and serve with almost unlimited expression. Married couples have a responsibility to each other and to their children that precludes this expression of freedom, those in religious communities live in obedience to superiors who determine assignments which precludes this expression of freedom, those living a hermit's life have physical boundaries that preclude this expression of freedom, and those who are ordained have responsibilities to their flock that preclude this expression of freedom. In a sense, only those living in the single state have a freedom of movement akin to consecrated virgins, though consecrated virgins are asked to bring major life decisions before their diocesan bishop to receive his counsel. It could also be said that consecrated virgins have a limit to movement precluded by the tie to the diocese, but it's also the case that consecrated virgins can retain this diocesan link while engaging in missionary works outside the diocese, or they may move to a different diocese for professional or personal reasons.

When we speak about freedom in this sense, it's not in a sense of being free from obligations, to be sure. Limits to freedom actually *free* us. With respect to the moral law, for example, moral norms allow us to operate within a boundary that has been set to allow our flourishing according to our nature and what God knows to be for our good. Freedom, in the context of the wide-ranging freedom of consecrated virginity, is a freedom to be always ready to follow the Lord wherever He leads.

In my own discernment of consecrated virginity, I remember feeling excitement thinking about the lack of certainty regarding the future. Most people, or at least those in my social circle, would look at uncertainty regarding their futures and be disturbed by it, or struggle to remain peaceful about not knowing when they would be married, whether their career would require them to move, how they might have to juggle caring for an elderly parent with a family of their own. However, whenever I would think of the future that existed as a blank slate, even if there was some relative sense of where things might be headed, I had a deep sense of excitement and peace about the adventure of it all. To be available to the Lord in every moment, to go where He sends me or do what He wants me to do, was and still is irresistibly attractive. My life today looks absolutely nothing like I thought it might when I received the consecration, and I have no idea where the Lord will continue taking me, but there is something beautiful about being radically available to Him in every moment.

One last point about living "in the world." The embedded witness of the consecrated virgin brings into the ordinary contexts of everyday life a soul that is wed to God. In doing so, she reveals how every small thing done for God becomes holy and sanctifying. Her living witness bears particular force in speaking to the possibility of being fulfilled completely by Christ and of not needing to reduce happiness to romantic or sexual fulfillment. By her life, she reveals that the impulses of human sexuality have many ways of directing us to communion with others, and that integrated sexuality can be holy, even in celibacy, and even in a culture that tends toward use instead of love. The consecrated virgin can be a profound witness of the communion of friendships, the communion of parish families, the communion of believers, and the communion and solidarity that can be found, simply put, person to person, when love is its impetus.

The Parable of the Wise and Foolish Virgins

The Parable of the Wise and Foolish Virgins speaks of the freedom to be ready to follow the Lord, but in it there are some strange things happening, as pointed out by Brant Pitre.[68] It starts with our understanding of Jewish marriage customs in the time of Jesus, which included the initial betrothal, after which time the couple would be considered married. However, they would not live together until the husband had readied their home and the marriage feast was given, which was typically seven days. During the marriage feast, a procession was held to the bridal chamber for the spouses to consummate their marriage. In Matthew 25:1–13, we read that the wise virgins, waiting for the Bridegroom to arrive, wouldn't share their oil with the foolish virgins. The passage seems to suggest that they were likely waiting not too far from vendors, since the feast would have taken part in the town or city that the

[68] Brant Pitre, "The Thirty-Second Sunday of Ordinary Time, Year A," *Catholic Productions*, accessed July 23, 2024, https://catholicproductions.com/blogs/mass-readings-explained-year-a/the-thirty-second-sunday-of-ordinary-time-year-a.

couple was from. The wise virgins seem to convey that it wouldn't have been impossible for the foolish ones to get their own oil easily. However, it is likely that the place where they were waiting for the Bridegroom would not have been far from the *chuppah*, the wedding chamber, and so the wise virgins would likely not have run out of oil had they shared it. Further, the wise virgins would have known that, because it was midnight when the Bridegroom came, that the vendors who could have supplied oil to the foolish virgins would be closed. Even more, when the foolish virgins *do* go to get oil and come back to the feast, the Bridegroom disavows *even knowing* them.

These seem like puzzling details. Why would the wise virgins not share when it may have been reasonable to share? Why are they called wise when their actions are not generous? Why does the Bridegroom shut out the foolish virgins, who would have been bridesmaids and either friends or relatives of the Bride? Would any groom not only do this, but seemingly disavow even knowing them?

As with other parables, Pitre suggests that it has to be seen both in its scriptural context and through the lens of the *nimshal* that accompanies it. A *nimshal* is "an explanation of the parable that drives home the main point."[69] We see Christ giving quite a long *nimshal* after the parable of the sower, for example. With the parable of the virgins, the story needs to be seen in the context of what surrounds it—parables on the kingdom of God. Therefore, understanding that this parable is speaking about entry into the kingdom of God, the details given are not so much about an earthly wedding feast as a heavenly one. The *nimshal* confirms this understanding with its short and to-the-point, "Therefore keep watch, because you do not know the day or the hour" (Matt. 25:13).

[69] Ibid.

This Scripture that is often associated with consecrated virginity, and even forms part of the symbology in the Rite of Consecration of a Virgin Living in the World, through the option of an oil lamp (the other option is a candle). It presents us with a deep ecclesial understanding that can be easily missed. In the passage's warning to be ready always for the coming of Christ, the wise virgins do indeed present an image of those who wait faithfully for the Bridegroom, and who ensure they do all in their power to follow Him without hesitation to the bridal chamber. Their single-heartedness and resistance to anything that could impede their role allows them to fulfill their duty to the Bridegroom. In the understanding of Jewish marriage ceremonies, the virgins from the Scripture were bridesmaids accompanying the Bridegroom and bride together to the bridal chamber. We can see, in this sense, that in addition to the bridal relationship that a consecrated virgin has with Christ, the parable gives another meaning to consecrated virginity in the Church, which is to usher in the consummation of the marriage between Christ, the Bridegroom, and the Bride, the Church.

St. Paul also gives us a powerful Scripture passage that gives light to what it means to be "in the world" in light of this task of walking souls to the Bridal Chamber of the Lamb. In 1 Corinthians, he says:

> Though I am free and belong to no one, I have made myself a slave to everyone, to win as many as possible. To the Jews I became like a Jew, to win the Jews. To those under the law I became like one under the law (though I myself am not under the law), so as to win those under the law. To those not having the law I became like one not having the law (though I am not free from God's law but am under Christ's law), so as to win those not having the law. To the weak I

> became weak, to win the weak. I have become all things to all people so that by all possible means I might save some. I do all this for the sake of the gospel, that I may share in its blessings. (1 Cor. 9:19-23)

The consecrated virgin can say this along with St. Paul. In her own person, she is free to become whatever the Lord is asking her to become. However, there is another aspect of this: the reality that consecrated virgins are members of an Order. It is an Order where its members are mystically bound together in the heart of their Spouse while they serve Him in their various dioceses across the world. In this way, and in a kind of reflection of the mystical reality of the Body of Christ, the Order of consecrated virgins can be "all things to all people."

Where Does the Consecrated Virgin Fit in the Universal and the Particular Church?

The terms universal and particular, in reference to the Church, refer to the whole Church (universal) and the diocesan Church or ecclesial body (particular; can include things like Ordinariates that are not necessarily geographically bounded as are most dioceses). These two aspects have a close interplay in the life of consecrated virgins in many respects. For example, the consecrated virgin fits into the universal Church by nature of her insertion into a true Order. In this sense, consecrated virgins are sisters of each other and share a close bond regardless of the diocese that each one is from, though her relationship to her bishop and diocese is always primary.

Another interplay can be seen with respect to charisms. Just as each religious order has a charism, within the *Ordo Virginum*, the charism is virginity.[70] In addition to this, the *Ordo* contains, in a sense, all charisms by virtue of the fact that each woman brings her own unique gifts into her diocesan life. These charisms are applied in the particular Churches, or at times are offered to a wider body, as through service with a national association or by providing assistance to the Dicastery for Institutes of Consecrated Life and Societies of Apostolic Life, which is the dicastery responsible for the *Ordo*. Regardless, the sum of the charisms given by the Holy Spirit to the individual members of the *Ordo* fulfills the mission of the *Ordo Virginum* as a whole. Consecrated virgins offer their charisms to the whole Church by virtue of membership in the *Ordo*, and to the particular church by virtue of their diocesan insertion.

There are also expressions of regulation of consecrated virginity that are appropriate to various levels of ecclesial authority. In

[70] Note: There is some debate over a requirement for physical virginity and the interpretation of the prerequisite that a woman "has never been married and has never lived in public or open violation of chastity (*Ecclesiae Sponsae Imago*, no. 44; cf. *Praenotanda* of the *Rite of Consecration of a Virgin Living in the World*, 5a and 5b) in light of *Ecclesiae Sponsae Imago* no. 88. It states that "the call to give witness to the Church's virginal, spousal and fruitful love for Christ is not reducible to the symbol of physical integrity. Thus to have kept her body in perfect continence or to have practised the virtue of chastity in an exemplary way, while of great importance with regard to the discernment, are not essential prerequisites in the absence of which admittance to consecration is not possible." The interpretation of the Instruction and the judgement of *whether* and *when* a woman has been given the charism of virginity is proper to the diocesan bishop; it is not the intention of this book to comment on what falls under his authority. As with many aspects of consecrated virginity, it is likely that this and other important considerations will gain further clarity over time.

the matters of universal expression, such as with canon laws that apply to consecrated virgins, the appropriate ecclesial authority is the Holy See. With respect to admission to the *Ordo* and its life in the diocese, the bishop is the appropriate ecclesial authority. This fundamental role of the diocesan bishop is an important one, because consecrated virginity is a public vocation in the Church. This means that the Church, through the ecclesial authority of the bishop, has confirmed the charism of virginity in the woman and established her as a consecrated virgin with all consecrated virginity's rights and responsibilities. The bishop is also the appropriate ecclesial authority responsible for implementing in his diocese the norms regarding formation and governance of consecrated virginity that are given by the Holy See.

So how does the authority of the bishop manifest itself with respect to how a consecrated virgin lives and serves within the diocese? The bishop does not pass out assignments in a way analogous to the superior of a religious institute, but instead is asked to discern the gifts that each consecrated virgin brings to the table and to assist her in discerning where and how to put these gifts at the service of the diocesan Church. It is a benefit to the woman, the diocesan Church, and the bishop himself to take the time to discern such gifts, and this involves a good deal of intentionality:

> So that personal charisms can be recognised, accepted and lived in their authenticity, consecrated women let themselves be accompanied and supported by the Church in the ongoing exercise of humble discernment, in order to understand what the will of God might be for their lives (Rm 12:2). This involves interpreting intelligently and with evangelical wisdom the spiritual experience of each consecrated woman, keeping in mind her life history and

> situating her in the concrete ecclesial and social context in which she lives.[71]

Regardless of the external manifestation of the consecrated virgin's activities, she is called to be deeply integrated into the life of the diocese: "Since this form of consecrated life is inserted in the particular Church, the candidate will nurture her bonds with the ecclesial community, by means of the network of fraternal relationships that make up the ordinary fabric of daily ecclesial life, and also, when possible, by participating in significant diocesan events."[72] The service to the particular Church—and foundationally, the call to pray for the needs of the diocese—necessitates *knowing* the diocese and its people. Though the bishop of a diocese would hopefully involve consecrated virgins in diocesan activities and celebrations, consecrated virgins themselves should assume as a chosen responsibility the task of intentionally integrating themselves in parish and diocesan life.

The relationship of a consecrated virgin with her bishop and her diocese is also unique for several reasons; one of them is the way in which most women come to be associated with their diocese. A woman does not generally feel called to consecrated virginity in a diocese through "shopping around" (understood colloquially) among different dioceses as one might do with discerning a call to religious life by attending "come and see" weekends. Almost universally, consecrated virgins are consecrated in the diocese they are living in and have roots in:

> The women who receive this consecration are called to let charity shine through their lives, charity that is the principle

[71] *Ecclesiae Sponsae Imago*, no. 28.

[72] Ibid., no. 100.

of unity and holiness in the whole body of the Church. They remain inserted in that part of the people of God in which they already live and in the heart of which their vocational discernment and the preparation for their consecration is carried out. They are, in fact, bound by a special bond of love and mutual belonging to this particular Church.[73]

Practical Applications: Responsibilities of Consecrated Virgins and Bishops

There are many practical questions regarding the relationship between the consecrated virgins and their bishops, and many of these are still being ironed out. Many things simply depend on the bishop himself, and on his level of desire and his ability to be closely involved with the life of the *Ordo Virginum* in his diocese. However, there are some normative responsibilities that *Ecclesiae Sponsae Imago* outlines for both bishops and consecrated virgins.

Consecrated virgins have responsibilities to:

- respect the magisterium of the diocesan bishop and accept his pastoral decisions with "intelligence and creativity"
- pray for the needs of the diocese, especially the intentions of the bishop
- develop relationships with other consecrated virgins in order to support each other and together support the needs of the diocese
- pray for deceased consecrated virgins
- and place their gifts at the disposal of the diocese and discern with the bishop how they are to serve[74]

[73] Ibid., no. 42.

[74] Ibid., nos. 43–44.

The diocesan bishop has a responsibility to:

- welcome vocations to consecrated virginity
- confer the consecration
- foster conditions "so that the insertion of consecrated women in the Church entrusted to him will contribute to the path of holiness and the mission of the people of God"
- foster pastoral concern for members of the *Ordo* and exercise his ministry of teaching, governing, and sanctifying with care of the consecrated virgins in mind
- express his fatherly love for consecrated virgins and give his encouragement to them so that they are able to live "in joyful fidelity to their own vocation"
- support the communion of members of the *Ordo virginum* through promoting regular gatherings and formation
- discern with the women and the whole *Ordo* regarding the ways in which the women will place their gifts at the service of the local Church
- encourage connection of the women with those in the *Ordo virginum* in other dioceses[75]

There is also a prophetic nature to the relationship between consecrated virgins and their bishops. In the diocesan Church, they can assist bishops in discerning where God is moving within the diocese, and thereby help him to accomplish the ecclesial ministry which is set out before him. This ability comes both from the consecrated virgin's deep life of prayer with the Lord and through her intimate knowledge of the people and needs of the diocese, especially within her spheres of parish life and the particular ministries that have been entrusted to her. *Vita consecrata* affirms this reality:

[75] Ibid., nos. 46–49.

> In the history of the Church, alongside other Christians, there have been men and women consecrated to God who, through a special gift of the Holy Spirit, have carried out a genuinely prophetic ministry, speaking in the name of God to all, even to the Pastors of the Church. *True prophecy is born of God*, from friendship with him, from attentive listening to his word in the different circumstances of history. Prophets feel in their hearts a burning desire for the holiness of God and, having heard his word in the dialogue of prayer, they proclaim that word with their lives, with their lips and with their actions, becoming people who speak for God against evil and sin. Prophetic witness requires the constant and passionate search for God's will, for self-giving, for unfailing communion in the Church, for the practice of spiritual discernment and love of the truth.[76]

Through the movements at play in individual dioceses, the prophetic voice of consecrated virgins can also impact the universal Church as She discerns the global movements of the Holy Spirit seen first in the particular Churches.

[76] *Vita consecrata*, no. 84.

Questions and Scriptures for Reflection

1. What elements of consecrated life resonate most with you?

2. Are there any elements of consecrated virginity that resonate with you?

3. How would you describe the vocation of consecrated virginity to someone?

4. How would you describe the way all vocations fit together in the Body of Christ?

5. How would you describe your relationship to your diocese? To your bishop?

Matthew 25:1–13
1 Corinthians 9:19–23
1 Corinthians12:4–14
Hebrews 10:19–25

4

Theologies of Celibacy and Virginity

Holy Virginity and that perfect chastity which is consecrated to the service of God is without doubt among the most precious treasures which the Founder of the Church has left in heritage to the society which He established.[77]

From the very beginning of the Church there have been men and women who have renounced the great good of marriage to follow the Lamb wherever he goes, to be intent on the things of the Lord, to seek to please him, and to go out to meet the Bridegroom who is coming. Christ himself has invited certain persons to follow him in this way of life, of which he remains the model.[78]

Terminology

Several terms are used to describe what Christ institutes in Matthew 19:12, but primarily these are virginity, celibacy, or continence tied

[77] Pope Pius XII, *Sacra virginitas* (On Consecrated Virginity) (March 25, 1954), no. 1, https://www.vatican.va/content/pius-xii/en/encyclicals/documents/hf_p-xii_enc_25031954_sacra-virginitas.html.

[78] *Catechism of the Catholic Church*, no. 1618.

to the qualifier "for the sake of the kingdom of heaven" or "for the sake of the kingdom of God" (Luke 18:29). In Scripture and the writings of the Fathers, the term virginity is almost universally used because it describes the state of the person who has renounced marriage for the sake of the kingdom. It was predominantly used as a descriptor for women because of the close association of virginity with never having married, but it also distinguished women who had never married from widows who chose to remain unmarried following the death of a spouse, and who had their own Order in the early Church. As we'll see later, there is also a significant meaning that the Church Fathers associated with the witness of integral virginity.

Over time, and as religious orders took shape, the term virginity for the sake of the kingdom was still largely used, but the term celibacy for the sake of the kingdom came to be used somewhat interchangeably. In some sense, it was more inclusive in its description of consecrated life, because consecrated life included many widows who joined religious orders after the death of their spouse. It also coincided with the Rite of Consecration of a Virgin largely going into disuse. Though most men and women who entered religious orders over time were virgins, the entrance requirement for virginity has also varied greatly over time, and contemporary religious orders generally don't automatically exclude an inquirer if virginity is not present. These two terms, virginity and celibacy, are now used essentially interchangeably, though it could be argued that celibacy for the sake of the kingdom properly describes consecrated life overall, and virginity for the sake of the kingdom properly describes consecrated virginity.

The final term, notably used by John Paul II in *A Theology of the Body*, is continence for the sake of the kingdom. We'll come back to this term later because of its connection to enabling celibate love through self-mastery. Continence for the sake of the kingdom describes not so much a state, but a *way* of being that directs the expression and way of loving of the person who is living "for the sake of the kingdom."

In this chapter (and for the rest of the book after it), I'll use the term "celibacy for the sake of the kingdom" where I'm referring to a common characteristic or theology pertinent to all forms of consecrated life. Where something is specific to consecrated virginity, or where it's helpful to examine how a particular point expresses itself in consecrated virginity, I'll use the term "virginity for the sake of the kingdom."

Matthew 19: Eunuchs "for the Sake of the Kingdom of Heaven"

In a previous chapter, we looked at the history of consecrated virginity, and we saw that it developed against a backdrop of the Jewish understanding of virginity, which was largely aimed at its preservation until marriage, and the associated negative perceptions toward perpetual virginity. Some exceptions included women who took private vows of virginity, men and women who took Nazirite vows, and the community of the Essenes. However, Christ's words on celibacy for the sake of the kingdom give a new and radical meaning to celibacy. St. Methodius describes the new vision of celibacy this way:

> For truly by a great stretch of power the plant of virginity was sent down to men from heaven, and for this reason it was not revealed to the first generations. For the race of mankind was still very small in number; and it was necessary that it should first be increased in number, and then brought to

> perfection.... God no longer allowed Man to remain in the same ways, considering how they might now proceed from one point to another, and advance nearer to heaven, until, having attained to the very greatest and most exalted lesson of virginity, they should reach to perfection."[79]

The foundational teaching regarding consecrated life, given in the words of Christ Himself, is found in the Gospel according to Matthew:

> Some Pharisees came to him to test him. They asked, "Is it lawful for a man to divorce his wife for any and every reason?" "Haven't you read," he replied, "that at the beginning the Creator 'made them male and female,' and said, 'For this reason a man will leave his father and mother and be united to his wife, and the two will become one flesh'? So they are no longer two, but one flesh. Therefore what God has joined together, let no one separate." "Why then," they asked, "did Moses command that a man give his wife a certificate of divorce and send her away?" Jesus replied, "Moses permitted you to divorce your wives because your hearts were hard. But it was not this way from the beginning. I tell you that anyone who divorces his wife, except for sexual immorality, and marries another woman commits adultery." The disciples said to him, "If this is the situation between a husband and wife, it is better not to marry." Jesus replied, "Not everyone can accept this word, but only those to whom it has been given. For there are eunuchs who were

[79] Methodius of Olympus, *The Banquet of the Ten Virgins*, Discourse I, New Advent, no. 2, accessed July 10, 2024, https://www.newadvent.org/fathers/062301.htm.

> born that way, and there are eunuchs who have been made eunuchs by others—and there are those who choose to live like eunuchs for the sake of the kingdom of heaven. The one who can accept this should accept it." (19:3–11)

The term that Jesus uses here—eunuchs—is a reference to men, specifically. In the first instance, it refers to men who were born with physical defects or who experienced impotence, which in both cases would mean they couldn't engage in the sexual act. The second case refers to those who had been castrated for some purpose, such as retaining a falsetto voice for musical purposes in court or for overseeing women in a harem. In the third case we find something very new: Christ reveals that there are some who choose to live like eunuchs and not marry. However, He attaches two conditions to this: that these persons have been "given" this "word," and that such persons choose to refrain from marriage "for the sake of the kingdom of Heaven."

The first of these conditions is that celibacy for the sake of the kingdom is a charism. *Ecclesiae Sponsae Imago* captures this right in its opening paragraph: "Responding to a charism kindled in them by the Holy Spirit, they [consecrated virgins] experience the spiritual fertility of an intimate relationship with him [Christ] and offer the fruits of this relationship to the Church and to the world."[80] We see here a direct echo of Christ's words—there are some "to whom [the gift of celibacy/virginity] has been given."

Virginity and celibacy are themselves charisms—gifts given by the Holy Spirit for the sanctification of the receiver and the building up of the Church. Though it is necessary to have received at least the charism of celibacy in order to enter into consecrated life,

[80] *Ecclesiae Sponsae Imago*, no. 1.

there are some to whom the charism of virginity has been given as a specific expression of celibacy for the sake of the kingdom. The charism of virginity is not simply about being and staying a virgin, but rather having safeguarded virginal integrity, it is the reception of the ability to persevere in holy virginity for one's whole life. St. Thomas Aquinas and St. Bonaventure echo this: virginity cannot be a gift received and lived for the sake of the kingdom unless there is a vow to keep it forever intact.[81]

A charism is also fundamentally different than a state. Simply because someone is born a virgin (which we all are) and has remained a virgin (which many do) does not mean that the Lord has given the charism of virginity as if by default. In fact, the writings of the Fathers strongly disagree with this thought. St. Augustine is insistent that holy virginity is not something to be reduced to esteem of bodily integrity alone divorced from intention: "For neither is [virginity] itself also honored because it is virginity, but because it has been dedicated to God, and, although it be kept in the flesh, yet is it kept by religion and devotion of the Spirit. And by this means even virginity of body is spiritual, which continence of piety vows and keeps."[82] Both celibacy for the sake of the kingdom, which is also a lifelong renunciation of sexual relations, and virginity for the sake of the kingdom are "not restricted to a mere 'no', but contains a profound 'yes' in the spousal order: the gift of self for love in a total and undivided manner."[83] Celibacy for the sake of the kingdom requires a free choice to receive and live the charism of celibacy or virginity that has been given.[84]

[81] See *Sacra virginitas*, no. 16.

[82] Augustine, *Of Holy Virginity*, no. 8.

[83] *Mulieris dignitatem*, no. 20.

[84] *Sacra virginitas*, no. 12.

One of the things that I experienced in my own vocational discernment is directly related to this concept of charisms. In Scripture, we are instructed to "test them all; hold on to what is good" (1 Thes. 5:21). The *Catechism* refers to this passage when it says:

> It is in this sense that discernment of charisms is always necessary. No charism is exempt from being referred and submitted to the Church's shepherds. "Their office [is] not indeed to extinguish the Spirit, but to test all things and hold fast to what is good," so that all the diverse and complementary charisms work together "for the common good."[85]

Since celibacy and virginity are charisms, they are not something that we declare we have autonomously received. It is the Church, in her various authorities, who discerns with us to authenticate what we believe are charisms that we have received.

It was a frustrating experience for me at several points in my vocational discernment to come up against this reality. When I was discerning religious life, I was told by a community that I loved dearly that they didn't sense a call in me for their community's charism, though they affirmed that this did not mean I didn't have a call to consecrated life in another community or form. At the time, I felt angry with God, and even felt somewhat betrayed. I felt like He was calling me to a spousal form of relationship with Him, but then He was shutting every door that I was trying to go through. It was incredibly painful to feel so drawn to give myself completely to Him and then to experience what felt like rejection.

However, because of the faithfulness of the Church, in the form of those discerning on her behalf with the communities I visited, I was able to allow the Lord to open my heart to the possibility of

[85] CCC, no. 801.

consecrated virginity. The prudent and careful listening that the vocation directresses exhibited ultimately led to my discovery of consecrated virginity, which is exactly the perfect fit for how the Lord has created my heart to love. Not only that, but through the process of discernment, I was also able to have a very clear sense that I *wasn't* called to religious life so that I could give a free yes to consecrated virginity; the Lord knew all along that I would need to enter into consecrated virginity knowing that I had discerned all the vocations well and had truly opened myself to all things so that He could show me *how* He wanted me to become His. Careful discernment on the part of the person *and* the competent Church authority is truly a gift from the Lord, both for the person and for the Church.

We can speak now of the second part of Christ's words on celibacy for the kingdom: if a charism is a gift received from the Holy Spirit for the sanctification of the person and the building up of the kingdom, there must be a means to use that charism. For example, if one receives a gift of prophecy, that gift is used to prophesy. In the case of celibacy, it is used "for the sake of the kingdom." Celibacy at the service of building the kingdom of God is the normative expression of the charism, which is remarkably wide, and as we'll see later, has a particular wideness in the vocation of consecrated virginity.

Celibacy, as a gift received, is an intentional "for"—it is "for" the kingdom of God and of Heaven. The kingdom of God, simply put, is where Christ reigns as King. This means, then, that the kingdom of Heaven is both here and coming; it is coming in the sense of the end of time when Christ will reign in victory over all things, and it is here now in the sense that where the love of God is, the eternal realities are present.[86] In other words, when we speak of celibacy for

86 Ratzinger, "Gift in the Church."

the sake of the kingdom, we mean that it is a gift received to allow one to live a life that incarnates Christ in the world and makes His love, His kingdom and His reign present, even now.

Since the kingdom of Heaven is here but also coming, a charism of celibacy or virginity is a living anticipation of the eternal kingdom where Christ will reign forever. Since the kingdom, both coming and already here, is directly connected to the presence and action of Christ, in its deepest essence, living out the charism of virginity means to give oneself without reserve not to a nebulous "thing," but to a Person: Christ Himself.[87] "Christian virginity," says Cardinal Ratzinger in a 1988 homily he gave at a consecration Mass, "is a spousal mystery, a quest for the true beauty which pleases Jesus the King."[88] Those who have been given the charism of virginity as consecrated virgins are called to become one with Christ, spouses of Christ, and to bring into this world the presence of Christ and the reign of His kingdom.

1 Corinthians 7: Anxious for the Affairs of the Lord

Apart from the earliest expressions of celibacy for the sake of the kingdom seen in John the Baptist, Our Lady and St. Joseph, and Jesus Himself, we see some other biblical witnesses who are beginning to live this teaching of Christ. The most explicit explanation in Scripture is arguably given by St. Paul, who begins to unfold much of the deeper meaning of refraining from marriage for the sake of the kingdom, explicitly extending it to both men and women. In chapter 7 of First Corinthians, he writes:

[87] *Ecclesiae Sponsae Imago,* no. 15.

[88] Ratzinger, "Gift in the Church."

Now in regard to the matters about which you wrote: "It is a good thing for a man not to touch a woman," but because of cases of immorality every man should have his own wife, and every woman her own husband. The husband should fulfill his duty toward his wife, and likewise the wife toward her husband. A wife does not have authority over her own body, but rather her husband, and similarly a husband does not have authority over his own body, but rather his wife. Do not deprive each other, except perhaps by mutual consent for a time, to be free for prayer, but then return to one another, so that Satan may not tempt you through your lack of self-control. This I say by way of concession, however, not as a command. Indeed, I wish everyone to be as I am, but each has a particular gift from God, one of one kind and one of another. Now to the unmarried and to widows I say: it is a good thing for them to remain as they are, as I do, but if they cannot exercise self-control they should marry, for it is better to marry than to be on fire....

Now in regard to virgins I have no commandment from the Lord, but I give my opinion as one who by the Lord's mercy is trustworthy. So this is what I think best because of the present distress: that it is a good thing for a person to remain as he is. Are you bound to a wife? Do not seek a separation. Are you free of a wife? Then do not look for a wife. If you marry, however, you do not sin, nor does an unmarried woman sin if she marries; but such people will experience affliction in their earthly life, and I would like to spare you that.

I tell you, brothers, the time is running out. From now on, let those having wives act as not having them, those weeping as not weeping, those rejoicing as not rejoicing,

> those buying as not owning, those using the world as not using it fully. For the world in its present form is passing away.
>
> I should like you to be free of anxieties. An unmarried man is anxious about the things of the Lord, how he may please the Lord. But a married man is anxious about the things of the world, how he may please his wife, and he is divided. An unmarried woman or a virgin is anxious about the things of the Lord, so that she may be holy in both body and spirit. A married woman, on the other hand, is anxious about the things of the world, how she may please her husband. I am telling you this for your own benefit, not to impose a restraint upon you, but for the sake of propriety and adherence to the Lord without distraction.
>
> If anyone thinks he is behaving improperly toward his virgin, and if a critical moment has come and so it has to be, let him do as he wishes. He is committing no sin; let them get married. The one who stands firm in his resolve, however, who is not under compulsion but has power over his own will, and has made up his mind to keep his virgin, will be doing well. So then, the one who marries his virgin does well; the one who does not marry her will do better.
>
> A wife is bound to her husband as long as he lives. But if her husband dies, she is free to be married to whomever she wishes, provided that it be in the Lord. She is more blessed, though, in my opinion, if she remains as she is, and I think that I too have the Spirit of God. (1 Cor. 7:1–9, 25–40, NABRE)

Paul's writings are situated within a backdrop of Christianity that expected the return of the Lord to be imminent. In this case, heeding Christ's words was, for Paul and others, an expression of faith in Christ's teaching regarding Eternal Life, where "people will neither marry nor be given in marriage" (Matt. 22:30). It makes sense in light of Paul's writing that, as "the appointed time has grown short," he would counsel Christians—at lease those who are able to without sin—to remain as they are, in expectation of Christ's return and the coming reality where marriage does not exist as it does in this life. It becomes, in some sense, an even more forceful witness to Christ, since Paul's pointing to Eternal Life is done against the backdrop of a variable belief in the afterlife among different sects of Jews.

Paul's lauding of those who "remain as they are" (1 Cor. 7–8, NABRE) is not relegated to the experience of the early Church. Those called to live celibacy for the kingdom in our times are invited to live in the same spirit of joyful expectation that the early Christians were called to by Paul. Those given the gift of being "anxious for the things of the Lord" (1 Cor. 7:32, NABRE) are an ever-present reminder of the call to all Christians to "stay awake" (Matt. 24:42, NABRE) and to watch for Christ's return.

Ephesians 5: The Great Analogy

In Ephesians, we find Paul speaking of what John Paul II calls the Great Analogy regarding human and divine marriage:

> Wives, submit yourselves to your own husbands as you do to the Lord. For the husband is the head of the wife as Christ is the head of the church, his body, of which he is the Savior. Now as the church submits to Christ, so also wives should submit to their husbands in everything. Husbands, love your wives, just as Christ loved the church and gave himself up for her to make her holy, cleansing her by

> the washing with water through the word, and to present her to himself as a radiant church, without stain or wrinkle or any other blemish, but holy and blameless. In this same way, husbands ought to love their wives as their own bodies. He who loves his wife loves himself. After all, no one ever hated their own body, but they feed and care for their body, just as Christ does the church—for we are members of his body. "For this reason a man will leave his father and mother and be united to his wife, and the two will become one flesh" [cf. Gen 2:24]. This is a profound mystery—but I am talking about Christ and the church. (Eph. 5:22–32)

The marriage analogy is presented over and over in Scripture, from the Old Testament where Israel is compared to an unfaithful bride, to the end, where the book of Revelation speaks of the Divine Bridegroom and His Bride, the Church (cf. Jer. 2:2; Eph. 5:22–33; Hos. 2:14–23; Rev. 19:6–8; Rev. 21:2; 22:17). Those members of the Church who live consecrated lives, and in particular consecrated women, share in a special way in this image, because they reveal in their own persons the identity of the Church, which is Bride. The Church, as we see in the history of consecrated virginity, has affirmed from its earliest days that women who are called to celibacy for the sake of the kingdom are spouses of Christ and constitute an image of the very relationship between Christ and the Church:

> Women who receive virginal consecration in the Church also draw on this mystery [the marriage of Christ and the Church]. For love of Christ, who is supremely loved, they renounce the experience of human matrimony to be united with him with a spousal bond, to experience and to give witness in the virginal condition (1 Cor 7:34) to the fruitfulness of this union, anticipating the reality of

> definitive communion with God to which all humanity is called (Lk 20:34–36).[89]

Trinitarian and Eucharistic Love

Celibacy for the sake of the kingdom is eschatological; it points, through its living reality of renunciation of marriage in this life, to the spousal reality that all are called to in eternal life. Truly, the dead born anew into eternity are called "virgins" (Rev. 14:4).[90] We will explore this theme more directly in a subsequent chapter. The spousal nature of celibacy for the sake of the kingdom is also trinitarian in its essence and sign:

> The *chastity* of celibates and virgins, as a manifestation of dedication to God with *an undivided heart* (cf. 1 Cor 7:32–34), is a reflection of the *infinite love* which links the three Divine Persons in the mysterious depths of the life of the Trinity, the love to which the Incarnate Word bears witness even to the point of giving his life, the love "poured into our hearts through the Holy Spirit" (Rom 5:5), which evokes a response of total love for God and the brethren.[91]

Fr. Raniero Cantalamessa quotes St. Gregory Nazianzen saying, "The first virgin is the Holy Trinity."[92]

What does this mean? Love, its very substance, exists in the Trinity in a communion of persons: the Lover (the Father), the Beloved (the Son), and the Love between them (the Holy Spirit).

89 *Ecclesiae Sponsae Imago*, no. 18.

90 See Ibid., no. 16.

91 *Vita consecrata*, no. 21.

92 Cantalamessa, *Virginity: A Positive Approach*, 16.

It is virginal because it is wholly undivided and complete. Fr. Cantalamessa illustrates this by comparing the reality of Trinitarian love to marital love, its image. He says that in marriage there is always some element of selfishness and desire, because spouses fulfill each other, but the persons of the Trinity are already perfectly happy because their love is completely gratuitous.[93] Renunciation of marriage for the sake of the kingdom, and in particular virginity for the sake of the kingdom, contains within it an image of the Divine Love of the Holy Trinity, as well as the ability to reveal Man's inherent call to gratuitous love. *Ecclesiae Sponsae Imago* puts it this way:

> The charism of virginity, accepted by the woman and confirmed by the Church through consecration, is a gift that derives from the Father, by means of the Son, in the Spirit. This gift safeguards, purifies, heals and increases the capacity of the person to love. It draws back into unity every fragment of her history and the various dimensions of her humanity—spirit, soul and body—so that she might be able to respond to this grace with the undivided, free and joyful commitment of her own existence.[94]

Rooted in and made possible by the Holy Trinity, celibacy, and especially virginity, for the sake of the kingdom is also profoundly Marian. "The day of the Annunciation of the Lord to the Virgin Mary is the origin of Christian virginity: it is born in the moment of the 'Yes' of the Virgin to the divine maternity."[95] The 'yes' of Our Lady is the inaugural moment of virginity lived for the sake of the

93 See Ibid., 17.

94 *Ecclesiae Sponsae Imago,* no. 23.

95 Ratzinger, "Gift in the Church."

kingdom and gives to Christian virginity the new understanding that Christ Himself speaks of during His ministry.

Virginity for the sake of the kingdom is also profoundly eucharistic. Pope Benedict XVI says this beautifully:

> Here I wish to reaffirm the importance of the witness of virginity, precisely in relation to the mystery of the Eucharist. In addition to its connection to priestly celibacy, the eucharistic mystery also has an intrinsic relationship to consecrated virginity, inasmuch as the latter is an expression of the Church's exclusive devotion to Christ, whom she accepts as her Bridegroom with a radical and fruitful fidelity. In the Eucharist, consecrated virginity finds inspiration and nourishment for its complete dedication to Christ.[96]

We can see this connection very directly in the Mass; pronouncing the words of Christ, the priest says, "This is my body, given up for you," and with her whole self given completely to Christ, the Christian virgin says this with her life.

Renunciation and Fulfillment

Now we turn to the final characteristics in our overview. We know that celibacy for the sake of the kingdom involves a renunciation of marriage and a family of one's own, as John Paul II writes in *A Theology of the Body*: "Man is able to choose the personal gift of self to another person in the conjugal covenant, in which they become

[96] Benedict XVI, *Sacramentum caritatis* (February 22, 2007), no. 81, https://www.vatican.va/content/benedict-xvi/en/apost_exhortations/documents/hf_ben-xvi_exh_20070222_sacramentum-caritatis.html.

'one flesh,' and he is also able to renounce freely such a gift of self to another person, in order that by choosing continence 'for the kingdom of heaven' he may give himself totally to Christ."[97] However, similar to the need for intentionality in the "for" of celibacy for the sake of the kingdom, the renunciation of marriage and family is a denial of self done in order to pick up one's cross, to follow the Lord more closely, and to love more widely.[98] It also requires an understanding of the goodness of what one is renouncing; the beauty of marriage is explicitly spoken of in the homily of the Rite of Consecration in order to highlight the good being renounced, both to affirm the great value of marriage and family and to affirm the great value of consecrated virginity.[99]

Interestingly, it's also important for celibates not to view their vocation in terms solely of what is given up, as though celibacy entails somehow an antithesis of fulfillment. In a very real sense, celibacy for the kingdom is a living of the greatest fullness of human experience, since in eternal life there is no human marriage, but only the marriage of the soul with Christ. In this sense, "chastity is not a denial of sex. It is an orientation of sexuality, of the whole vital instinct, towards a desired finality."[100] Fr. Raniero Cantalamessa even goes so far as to say that celibacy is not renouncing marriage, but rather a renunciation of a lifelong commitment to a creature in order to commit eternally to the Uncreated One; it's not surrendering a concrete love for an

97 John Paul II, *Man and Woman He Created Them*, no. 80.6.

98 Ibid., 79.4.

99 John Paul II, *Man and Woman He Created Them*, no. 81.3; cf. "Homily," in *Rite of Consecration of a Virgin Living in the World* (May 31, 1970), no. 16.

100 Erik Varden, *Chastity: Reconciliation of the Senses* (Bloomsbury Continuum, 2023), 15.

abstract one, but relinquishing one person for another who is "infinitely more real."[101]

Part of this gift of living the fullfilment of eternity in this world comes in the ability of those who are celibate for the sake of the kingdom to follow Christ more closely. During the profession of perpetual vows in a religious order, the superior will often receive the vows of poverty, chastity, and obedience and then give a statement similar to this: "I receive your vows with joy.... Should you persevere in faithfully observing them, you are assured eternal life." In Judaism, around the time of Christ, being a disciple of a Rabbi entailed following the Rabbi so closely that everything about him would be taken on by the disciple—his mannerisms, his appearance, and even how he walked. The ability to imitate the poor, chaste, and obedient Christ, which is made more immediately possible in consecrated life as the disciple "is worried about the things of the Lord," breeds in the person the holiness of the One who is followed, even to the point of crucifixion and death, whether that comes spiritually or bodily. "In truth, virginity gives souls a force of spirit capable of leading them even to martyrdom, if needs be: such is the clear lesson of history which proposes a whole host of virgins to our admiration, from Agnes of Rome to Maria Goretti."[102]

The renunciation of marriage and family, and the closer following of Christ, brings with it a freedom to love widely, and to be "concerned about the Lord's affairs," as St. Paul says (1 Cor. 7:32). This is not to say in any way that those who are married cannot also love self-sacrificially and profoundly, but rather that

> the Apostle is ... asserting clearly that their hearts [the hearts of husbands and wives] are divided between love of

[101] Cantalamessa, *Virginity: A Positive Approach*, 23–24.

[102] *Sacra virginitas*, no. 28.

> God and love of their spouse, and beset by gnawing cares, and so by reason of the duties of their married state they can hardly be free to contemplate the divine. For the duty of the married life to which they are bound clearly demands: "They shall be two in one flesh." For spouses are to be bound to each other by mutual bonds both in joy and in sorrow. It is easy to see, therefore, why persons who desire to consecrate themselves to God's service embrace the state of virginity as a liberation, in order to be more entirely at God's disposition and devoted to the good of their neighbor. How, for example, could a missionary such as the wonderful St. Francis Xavier, a father of the poor such as the merciful St. Vincent de Paul, a zealous educator of youth like St. John Bosco, a tireless "mother of emigrants" like St. Francis Xavier Cabrini, have accomplished such gigantic and painful labors, if each had to look after the corporal and spiritual needs of a wife or husband and children?[103]

The "Lord's affairs," it should be noted, are not always the apostolic works that we often think of but are primarily the sanctification of the world through the faithful observance of all that is entailed in consecrated life, especially in the ministry of intercession and offering of personal sufferings and penances. Pius XII puts it this way: "The fruit of virginity is not only in these external works, to which it allows one to devote oneself more easily and fully, but also in the earnest prayer offered for others and the trials willingly and generously endured for their sake, which are other very perfect forms of charity toward one's neighbor."[104]

[103] Ibid., no. 20.
[104] Ibid., no. 27.

Self-Mastery and Continence for the Sake of the Kingdom

John Paul II's preferred term for consecrated life—continence for the sake of the kingdom of Heaven—is the final term of the three that were identified in the initial part of this chapter. His writings on the consecrated life in *A Theology of the Body* are set in the context of building what he calls an "adequate [theological] anthropology" of Man.[105]

Foundationally, Man's original experiences reveal his call to communion. Through their creation as male and female, Adam and Eve discover through their physicality the meaning of their bodies, which John Paul II calls the spousal meaning of the body: the incarnated ability of human persons to exist in a dynamism of self-gift, and in doing so, to live fully the meaning of their own existence.[106] This spousal meaning of the body is not just in relation to sexuality in the context of marriage, but is fundamental to the human person. Thus, in the case of celibacy for the kingdom, the expression of the spousal meaning of the body is upheld through the pouring out of the person in self-gift to others and receiving the gift of others in return, and in doing so, to enter into a communion of persons.

Following the Fall, Man lives under the effects of concupiscence, which results in the obscuring of the spousal meaning of the body; the ability to perceive the full gift of the human person, and to enter into a communion of persons, is inhibited by our tendency toward sin. In marriage, this is summed up by God's pronouncement after the Fall, "Your desire will be for your husband and he will rule over you" (Gen. 3:16). In the wider net of relationships,

[105] John Paul II, *Man and Woman He Created Them*, no. 5.2.

[106] Ibid., no. 15.1.

the effect of the Fall means the general disorder of human desire which manifests itself in varying ways, and the tendency toward using others instead of loving them.

In the case of celibacy for the sake of the kingdom, there are many temptations against chastity and the proper expression of the spousal meaning of the body, just as there are for those who are single or married: emotional unchastity (a disordered emotional attachment to others), lust (whether involving a disordered thought life or acting on temptations with the self or others), treating others as objects (example, using pornography), etc. For celibates, the specific sacrifices made are of the goods of marriage, namely children, fidelity, and the sacramental bond. The goods of physical union are part of this sacrifice, but the desires associated with those goods remain. *Sacra virginitas* says, "The virtue of chastity does not mean that we are insensible to the urge of concupiscence, but that we subordinate it to reason and the law of grace, by striving wholeheartedly after what is noblest in human and Christian life."[107]

In contrast to falling into the thought that chastity, lived in any vocation, is about successfully repressing sexual urges, the *Catechism* says that chastity "means the successful integration of sexuality within the person."[108] In other words, we possess the virtue of chastity in the measure that our sexual desires, which are given in order to draw us to communion, are rightly ordered to communion and gift as opposed to use. In the life of a celibate person, this means that our sexual desires are still ordered to communion, but that communion is expressed differently and in a way that does not culminate in sexual union with another. Part

[107] *Sacra virginitas*, no. 35.
[108] CCC, no. 2337.

of the power of the consecrated life is that it is a witness against the prevailing culture, which sees the human person as a form of animal driven by instincts and urges, which John Paul II says is an entirely inadequate view of the human person who has been given the gift of reason and the freedom for choice.[109] *Vita consecrata* expresses this beautifully:

> The consecrated life must present to today's world examples of chastity lived by men and women who show balance, self-mastery, an enterprising spirit, and psychological and affective maturity. Thanks to this witness, human love is offered a stable point of reference: the pure love which consecrated persons draw from the contemplation of Trinitarian love, revealed to us in Christ. Precisely because they are immersed in this mystery, consecrated persons feel themselves capable of a radical and universal love, which gives them the strength for the self-mastery and discipline necessary in order not to fall under the domination of the senses and instincts. Consecrated chastity thus appears as a joyful and liberating experience.[110]

Gaudium et spes contains this profound statement: "Man, who is the only creature on earth which God willed for itself, cannot fully find himself except through a sincere gift of himself."[111] All of us, regardless of vocation, are called into a communion of love with others which is constituted by our ability to give ourselves away in love and to receive the love of others. However, and again pertaining to all persons regardless of vocation, original sin has

[109] John Paul II, *Man and Woman He Created Them,* no. 80.4.

[110] *Vita consecrata,* no. 88.

[111] *Gaudium et spes,* no. 24.

disordered the desires of our hearts such that we cannot freely give and receive love. For every person, there are desires of the heart that ought to be ordered to God and to love but are instead warped by sin and are ordered to the use of other persons. This looks different for each of us because we are unique individuals with unique experiences, unique wounds, and unique attachments to sin, and temptations to use others can also show up differently in different vocations. For example, it is possible for spouses to fall into lust and diminish conjugal union to something that is solely about sexual pleasure without regard for the other. In consecrated life, it is possible to respond to loneliness by engaging in imprudent relationships with others to feed one's need for companionship instead of depending on a deep union with the Lord that makes healthy friendship possible, where each person desires to love the other freely.

In all cases, what John Paul II identifies as the remedy to our disordered desires is self-mastery. Self-mastery means that we are not ruled by our emotions or desires, but rather that our desires are subject to our intellect and will such that we are not ruled by our passions. The *Catechism* puts it succinctly: "Chastity includes an *apprenticeship in self-mastery* which is a training in human freedom. The alternative is clear: either man governs his passions and finds peace, or he lets himself be dominated by them and becomes unhappy."[112] When we can come to a place of self-mastery, we become free to love because we are able to choose the good of the other over whatever selfish good our passions are suggesting has highest importance. Self-mastery does not necessarily mean that all our desires are once again completely ordered toward the good, because the Lord will work over the course of our whole life on

[112] CCC, no. 2339.

reordering those desires, but it does mean that growing in self-mastery can help us enter into communions of love with others, even when we feel the pull of selfishness.

This call to self-mastery for the enablement of freedom to love is why John Paul II prefers the term continence for the sake of the kingdom of Heaven: continence refers to the cardinal virtue of temperance, which allows us to make right use of our passions in accord with reason.[113] Continence for the sake of the kingdom of Heaven implies in the term that the person called to this state is called to self-mastery in order to love freely.

Practical Applications: Integrated Celibate Sexuality

Amidst all our brokenness and all the influences of the world that are contrary to chaste love, how can we cultivate self-mastery and the continence that allows us to love freely? With respect to the challenge of living perfect chastity, greater healing and wholeness give us greater freedom from compulsive or habitual sin because we can identify the roots of feelings and experiences that drive us to the coping mechanisms that we have developed in our lives. There are several very practical things that can aid in our healing and self-mastery.

The first is that temptations to use another person, and in particular temptations to lust, which strike at the core of the desires that call us to communion, have a root. There is a saying that goes like this: hurt people hurt people, and healed people heal people. In consecrated life we are called to love widely and to exercise a spiritual maternity, and we are free to do this in the measure that we ourselves are healed and whole.

[113] Ibid., no. 2341.

Psychologists and spiritual directors are both excellent, and I would even suggest, necessary resources for personal integration. Psychologists or psychotherapists can help us to understand and process how our current realities and formative experiences have affected the ways we think about and respond to ourselves, allowing us to gain the freedom to move from reactivity to responsivity in our lives. Understanding ourselves, and why we feel or react the way we do, can help us tremendously in gaining the freedom to interact with the world and ourselves through our free choices and not our impulses, which often spring from wounds. Spiritual directors, in addition to helping us hear what the Lord is speaking to us and how He is drawing us deeper in holiness, can also help us to see how Christ responds to our woundedness, and where He is bringing healing so that we are free to love others with a heart that is whole. A good spiritual director and a good psychotherapist will also know the boundaries of their own competency such that they can refer you to other professionals where needed. Often, the combination of spiritual direction and therapy is extremely helpful in the process of coming to interior integration.

Safeguarding our chastity is not simply about avoiding lustful thoughts or lustful actions with ourselves or another person, but it also involves the life of emotion—especially for women. This takes the form of what we might call emotional unchastity. If sins against chastity are described as the use of a person for selfish pleasure as opposed to loving a person through a praxis of self-gift, then emotional unchastity would be the use of persons to fulfill an emotional need. This is not the same as having friendships that are based in mutual love and sharing, but rather would be a distortion of friendship where self-gift becomes eclipsed by a selfish focus on self-fulfillment. Emotional unchastity is anything that places a relationship into the realm of realizing attractions in ways other than through physical fulfillment.

Unless there is same-sex attraction in the picture, emotional unchastity is more common between men and women, where emotional investment and vulnerability are abused in a way that seeks to usurp the fulfillment the Lord longs to give us Himself or through other well-ordered relationships. It would be seen, for instance, in a consecrated woman seeking to ameliorate an unaddressed problem of loneliness by entering into an imprudent relationship with a priest friend and seeking an emotional intimacy that mimics the emotional sharing present in a marriage.

To be sure, the line of emotional chastity can be difficult to navigate, because it is good and healthy for consecrated women to have friendships with our brother priests or other men, but we need to be extremely vigilant over our hearts in these relationships and always honest with ourselves about what we are seeking. This is especially important in moments of our spiritual lives where we experience desolation or dryness and the desire for intimacy increases. The Lord allows this desire to flower in us as a means of helping us to long for Him, but we can easily see how temptations to have this longing met could mistakenly direct us to seek intimacy with someone who is not the Lord, especially if He seems silent or distant. Warning signs for emotional unchastity might include things such as a desire for daily contact with the person, seeking opportunities to be alone together, or turning first to that person for emotional support when difficulties present themselves.

An excellent safeguard against this is to develop relationships with other consecrated women with whom you can check in regularly about the state of your heart and your relationship with the Lord, and who can act as accountability partners if you experience an attraction to a man or temptations toward emotional unchastity.

Spiritual directors are also excellent resources for things like this, and many saints recommend ensuring that the relationship with a spiritual director is one where you can pour out your heart freely. Also, then, it's important to make sure that if your spiritual director is male, that any sense of attraction toward him be taken seriously, and possibly a new spiritual director be found.

Turning back to safeguarding our chastity in general, there are also very practical means we can use. These means begin with avoiding elements we know contradict chastity, such as music, movies, and TV shows that contain elements contrary to chastity. Pius XII underscores this:

> In order to acquire this perfect mastery of the spirit over the senses, it is not enough to refrain from acts directly contrary to chastity, but it is necessary also generously to renounce anything that may offend this virtue nearly or remotely; at such a price will the soul be able to reign fully over the body and lead its spiritual life in peace and liberty.[114]

We know, though, that especially because the vocation of consecrated virginity is lived in the world, it means that we cannot withdraw from the world as completely as those in religious orders may be able to; therefore, there will likely be external and internal challenges to safeguarding our chastity. Another foundational help is simply to remember to flee! Pius XII comments on the counsel of St. Jerome and St. Augustine, and says:

> For the preserving of chastity, according to the teaching of Jerome, flight is more effective than open warfare: "Therefore I flee, lest I be overcome." Flight must be understood

[114] *Sacra virginitas*, no. 36.

> in this sense, that not only do we diligently avoid occasion of sin, but especially that in struggles of this kind we lift our minds and hearts to God, intent above all on Him to Whom we have vowed our virginity. "Look upon the beauty of your Lover," St. Augustine tells us.[115]

It is a good practice not to trust ourselves to avoid temptations against chastity, because our resolve can change according to many things: how tired we are, how strong the attack is, whether we are experiencing emotional upheaval, and even the natural rhythms and desires that are built into the body of a woman in support of procreation. In every case, when we experience temptations toward unchastity, whether external or interior, the wisest response is to flee from the temptation.

If there is a show we're watching that we discover has depictions of unchastity, flight is to immediately turn it off and not go back to it. If we are tempted to dwell on thoughts of how nice the embrace of a male friend would be in moments where we're lonely, flight would be to immediately ask the Lord's help to interrupt those thoughts and then to do something to distract ourselves. If we experience temptations to seek affirmations of our desirability or beauty by wearing clothing that is not entirely modest, flight would be throw out any inappropriate clothing and set rules for ourselves about what we will and won't purchase in the future. These may even seem like trivial examples, but because the beauty of virginal chastity is so powerful, do not underestimate the target that is on the back of those who abide in it. We need to give the enemy no footholds for attack, and the best way to do this is to flee from temptations straight away without entertaining them.

[115] Ibid., no. 54.

Apart from controlling what we take in and ensuring we flee from temptations, we can be proactive in our ability to safeguard our chastity through the normal (but very effective) means that the Church gives. Pope Pius XII recommends things that "surpass the powers of nature," which are prayer to God, regular confession and Mass, and a deep devotion to Our Lady.[116] The *Catechism* adds to this self-knowledge, the practice of mortifications to order our passions, obedience to God's commandments, and growing in the moral virtues (prudence, temperance, justice, and fortitude).[117] St. Augustine adds, "Say not that you have chaste minds though you may have wanton eyes, for a wanton eye is the index of a wanton heart."[118] Practicing custody of the eyes, which means turning our eyes away immediately from anything that is immodest or that we know may trigger lustful thoughts, is also necessary. One note about this: custody of the eyes doesn't mean we should be overly scrupulous and be afraid to look at the world around us for fear of temptations. The Lord simply asks us to be reasonably prudent with how we use our senses.

We should also remember that growth in virtue and the self-mastery of continence for the kingdom of Heaven is a life-long task that even requires varying approaches at different life stages because the challenges to chastity vary over time from things like our oscillating sexual drives (which for women vary even with something like menstrual cycles), to responding to the different experiences of loneliness or vulnerability as we age.[119] However, we

116 Ibid., no. 61.

117 CCC, no. 2340.

118 Augustine, *Letter 211*, no. 10, New Advent, accessed July 10, 2024, https://www.newadvent.org/fathers/1102211.htm.

119 CCC, no. 2342.

can end this chapter with the words of Pius XII and the Fathers who share these beautiful words about virginal chastity, in particular:

> For virginity is a difficult virtue; that one be able to embrace it there is needed not only a strong and declared determination of completely and perpetually abstaining from those legitimate pleasures derived from marriage; but also a constant vigilance and struggle to contain and dominate rebellious movements of body and soul, a flight from the importunings of this world, a struggle to conquer the wiles of Satan. How true is that saying of Chrysostom: "the root, and the flower, too, of virginity is a crucified life." For virginity, according to Ambrose, is as a sacrificial offering, and the virgin "an oblation of modesty, a victim of chastity." Indeed, St. Methodius, Bishop of Olympus, compares virgins to martyrs, and St. Gregory the Great teaches that perfect chastity substitutes for martyrdom: "Now, though the era of persecution is gone, yet our peace has its martyrdom, because though we bend not the neck to the sword, yet with a spiritual weapon we slay fleshly desires in our hearts." Hence a chastity dedicated to God demands strong and noble souls, souls ready to do battle and conquer "for the sake of the kingdom of heaven."[120]

[120] *Sacra virginitas*, no. 49.

Questions and Scriptures for Reflection

1. How would I explain the meaning of virginity to someone?

2. Have I received a charism of celibacy/virginity? How am I living this charism "for"—to make present even now—the kingdom of God?

3. What does it mean for me to witness to the hope of eternal life?

4. How do I experience self-mastery, and where might I be called to greater self-mastery?

5. Where might the Lord be calling me to greater healing and wholeness? Am I open to seeing the wounded parts of my own heart? What supports can I seek out and rely on?

Matthew 19:3–11
1 Corinthians 7:1–39
Ephesians 5:22–32
Matthew 22:30
Revelation 14:4
Luke 22:7–38

5

Theology of Eschatology and Witness

The custom of consecrating women to a life of virginity flourished even in the early Church. It led to the formation of a solemn rite constituting the candidate a sacred person, a surpassing sign of the Church's love for Christ, and an eschatological image of the world to come and the glory of the heavenly Bride of Christ.[121]

Virginity for the sake of the kingdom of heaven is an unfolding of baptismal grace, a powerful sign of the supremacy of the bond with Christ and of the ardent expectation of his return, a sign which also recalls that marriage is a reality of this present age which is passing away.[122]

The Sacramentality of the Celibate Body

This chapter focuses on what can be seen and understood in the witness of consecrated virginity. The eschatological meaning

[121] *Praenotanda*, in *Rite of Consecration of a Virgin Living in the World* (May 31, 1970), no. 1, https://diolc.org/files/consecratedlife/Complete%20Rite.pdf.

[122] CCC, no. 1619.

of celibacy for the sake of the kingdom refers to the revelation of eternal realities by those who are living them in an anticipatory way in this life. Eschatological, as an adjective, takes its meaning from the noun "eschaton," which is the end of time when Christ will come to judge the living and the dead and His kingdom will be fully realized. If something is an eschatological sign, it means that it points to a reality that will be present in the eschaton. In other words, an eschatological sign is something that reminds people of the final destination and experience of the human soul.

A helpful place to begin is to clarify what we mean when we're speaking about signs and sacraments in the Catholic Tradition. We have such a beautiful way of speaking of signs in the Church, but ultimately what we mean is that one thing reveals or points to something else. For example, when we use incense in liturgies it is a sign of our prayers ascending to God.

Sacraments are signs, but they go even further. The *Catechism* tells us that, "The sacraments are efficacious signs of grace, instituted by Christ and entrusted to the Church, by which divine life is dispensed to us. The visible rites by which the sacraments are celebrated signify and make present the graces proper to each sacrament."[123] What this means is that a sacrament brings into temporal reality something of the divine. For example, the sacrament of Confession is not just a sign of reconciliation with God and His Body, but it also *does* reconcile us with God and His Body.

In the strict sense of the term, there are seven sacraments which have been instituted by the Lord.[124] However, there

[123] CCC, no. 1131.
[124] Ibid., no. 1117.

are wider understandings of sacramentality that apply to the Church and the body. *Lumen gentium* speaks of the Church as a sacrament:

> Christ, having been lifted up from the earth has drawn all to Himself. Rising from the dead He sent His life-giving Spirit upon His disciples and through Him has established His Body which is the Church as the universal sacrament of salvation.[125]

In accord with the definition of a sacrament, we can see that the Church has a sacramental nature by virtue of her ability to bring divine life into the visible realm and to be a means through which grace is made available to the faithful.

In *Theology of the Body*, John Paul II speaks about the sacramental nature of the body: "The body, in fact, and only the body, is capable of making visible what is invisible: the spiritual and the divine. It has been created to transfer into the visible reality of the world, the mystery hidden from eternity in God, and thus to be a sign of it."[126] We can see here that the body also bears the marks of a kind of sacrament in accord with the same widened definition that applies to the Church—the body is a sign that reveals the very mysteries of God, but also possesses the ability to bring about the mysteries and kingdom of God in the world. To understand what can be comprehended through the sign of the celibate body, some other concepts from *Theology of the Body* form a helpful basis.

We spoke previously about the spousal meaning of the body, which is the incarnate ability of human persons to exist in a

[125] *Lumen gentium*, no. 9.

[126] John Paul II, *Man and Woman He Created Them*, no. 19.4.

dynamism of self-gift and, in doing so, to live fully the meaning of their own existence. This spousal understanding of the body is something that John Paul II comes to by looking back to "the beginning"—to Genesis and the creation narratives. He unfolds how Adam was created and discovered subjectivity (that he *is* a person) and solitude (that there is no other created being like him), and how this opened Adam up to the desire for communion with one like him. Upon the creation of Eve, Adam and Eve discover, in and through their bodies, that they were created for union and to enter a communion of persons where each makes a complete gift of self to the other and receives the gift of the other in turn. The fruit of their union is the life that comes forth; this fruitfulness that flows from communion is most often association with children flowing from marriage, but it also extends to the fruitfulness of all forms of human communion, such as spiritual motherhood in the case of consecrated women.

Paul says in Ephesians, "'For this reason a man will leave his father and mother and be united to his wife, and the two will become one flesh.' This is a profound mystery—but I am talking about Christ and the church" (Eph. 5:31–32). In this verse, Paul is showing us that human marriage is a sign of the heavenly marriage between Christ and the Church. In light of Christ's words regarding those who receive the gift of celibacy for the sake of the kingdom of Heaven, it becomes clear that those who receive this gift are a sign of the eternal marriage of the soul with Christ. In the way we love and live as celibates, and through the nature of our relationship with Christ, we are speaking a prophetic word about the meaning of the human person and about our destiny in eternal life. To explain this another way: our bodies, in their celibate state, oriented toward God in a spousal relationship, stand as a sign to those we encounter; through our spousal unity with

God in this life, we reveal that every soul is ultimately called to an exclusive spousal union with God.

There is also something that consecrated virginity has a particular power to point to. John Paul II writes that:

> Continence "for" the kingdom of heaven is certainly related to the revelation of the fact that "in" the kingdom of heaven "they take neither wife nor husband" (Matthew 22:30). It is a charismatic sign.... This way of existing as a human being (male and female) points out the eschatological "virginity" of the risen Man, in which, I would say, the absolute and eternal spousal meaning of the glorified body will be revealed in union with God Himself, but seeing Him "face to face," glorified moreover through the union of a perfect subjectivity that will unite all the "sharers in the other world," men and women, in the mystery of the communion of saints. Earthly continence "for the kingdom of God" is without doubt a sign that indicates this truth and this reality. It is a sign that the body, whose end is not death, tends toward glorification; already by this very fact it is, I would say, a testimony among men that anticipates the future resurrection.[127]

Breaking this down, what we see is that all persons will be virgins in Heaven since sacramental marriage (the sign that points to the union of Christ and His Bride, the Church) exists only in this life. Virginity, in this sense, refers to the total and exclusive communion with God in perfect purity that will be present in Heaven and that celibacy for the sake of the kingdom is a foretaste of here and now. Those celibates who already live the heavenly reality of

[127] Ibid., 75.1.

eternal virginity in this life are signs of the eternal virginity that all will share in. This is not simply a spiritual reality, but a whole-person, body and soul, reality, in which the whole being of the consecrated person is living an anticipated kind of bodily glorification whose trajectory reaches into eternal life already. Consecrated virginity constitutes a particularly compelling sign of the virginal reality of all who attain eternal life.

Practically speaking, in the almost unlimited ability of consecrated virgins to be present in the world, *precisely because* the vocation is lived in the world, there is another compelling sign present in a unique way in this vocation. Consecrated virgins are part of a worldwide *Ordo*, but without extinguishing the diocesan nature of consecrated virginity, and so reveal what the realities of heaven will be, where each of us will be completely united to God and each other without losing our own individuality. Consecrated virginity is a foreshadowing of the radical unity of all persons in Christ that will be fulfilled in eternity.

I remember at first being surprised by the joy of others and their expressions of love when it came up in conversations that I was in formation for consecrated virginity. It seemed to be disproportionate joy, in my inexperienced estimation. However, as I moved toward consecration and then afterwards, I realized that it was exactly the sign value of the consecration that was inspiring joy. There was something that people were obviously experiencing upon meeting someone who was staking her life on what comes *after* life, and who, in some way, was making visible the relationship that all souls long for, whether they know it or not.

This example is where we can also see the second part of the definition of a sacrament: it effects what it signifies. If the celibate body is a sign of the eternal realities, this means that one who is celibate for the sake of the kingdom can transfer into the visible reality of the world the invisible realities of eternal life. This may seem somewhat intangible, but there is a poem often attributed to John Henry Cardinal Newman that captures the sense of this dynamic:

> Stay with me, and then I shall begin to shine as Thou shinest: so to shine as to be a light to others. The light, O Jesus, will be all from Thee. None of it will be mine. No merit to me. It will be Thou who shinest through me upon others. O let me thus praise Thee, in the way which Thou dost love best, by shining on all those around me. Give light to them as well as to me; light them with me, through me. Teach me to show forth Thy praise, Thy truth, Thy will. Make me preach Thee without preaching—not by words, but by my example and by the catching force, the sympathetic influence, of what I do—by my visible resemblance to Thy saints, and the evident fulness of the love which my heart bears to Thee.[128]

It is the last lines that speak most to this experience; there is a "catching force" of the Holy Spirit within the consecrated person that speaks to unseen realities through the person who *is* seen. There is a particular way of being drawn up into the divine realities of the Holy Trinity that is expansive—those who live celibacy for the sake of the kingdom are not living an anticipation of eternity only for themselves. Since God is generous, they are living it in a way that opens the eternal realities to others who, through the gift of celibate love, are also drawn up into this divine communion.

[128] John Henry Cardinal Newman, "Jesus the Light of the Soul," in *Meditations and Devotions*, ed. Rev. W. P. Neville, pt. 3, no. 7.3, Newman Reader, accessed August 22, 2024, https://www.newmanreader.org/works/meditations/meditations10.html.

The Signs of Celibate Bridal Love: Virgin, Feminine, and Spousal

The witness of consecrated life is not primarily in relation to the apostolic works of one who is celibate for the sake of the kingdom, though, of course, the works that are carried out are part of the witness because they reveal the total dedication of the person to God and that person's freedom to pursue the works of God freely. If this were so, there would be no eschatological value assigned to cloistered or monastic life, which is certainly not the case. In terms of the uniqueness of witness, the *Ordo Virginum* stands out in the power it possesses to reveal that the union of the soul with Christ is not dependent on works, though works spring *from* the soul united to God. Every member of the *Ordo* has a life that looks different from other members, which means that the union with God *must* be about something more than what life consists of in day-to-day activities. The eschatological witness receives equal force in the life of the consecrated virgin who runs a diocesan office and in the life of a consecrated virgin in the later stages of her life who leaves her home infrequently and with much difficulty.

It is the reality of a consecrated virgin's spousal union with Christ, which pervades and animates every aspect of her life, that constitutes the witness and reveals the union that every soul will experience in eternity; this is even part of the examination during the Rite of Consecration when the bishop asks, "Are you so resolved to follow Christ in the spirit of the Gospel that your whole life may be a faithful witness to God's love and a convincing sign of the kingdom of heaven?"[129] *Vita consecrata* underscores this beautifully:

[129] "Examination," in *Rite of Consecration of a Virgin Living in the World*, chap. 1, no. 17.

> It is the duty of the *consecrated life* to show that the Incarnate Son of God is *the eschatological goal towards which all things tend*, the splendour before which every other light pales, and the infinite beauty which alone can fully satisfy the human heart. In the consecrated life, then, it is not only a matter of following Christ with one's whole heart, of loving him "more than father or mother, more than son or daughter" (cf. Mt 10:37)—for this is required of every disciple—but of living and expressing this *by conforming one's whole existence to Christ* in an all-encompassing commitment which foreshadows the eschatological perfection, to the extent that this is possible in time and in accordance with the different charisms.[130]

In addition to the eschatological sign that is given in the vocation of consecrated virginity are other revelations of divine life. Importantly, the consecrated virgin is, as a spouse of Christ, an image of the Church who is the definitive Spouse of Christ:

> The Church is virginal, feminine and spousal in relation to God, and these are things that the consecrated virgin lives in the sacramentality of her body such that she is a reality of virginity, femininity, and spousality in her person as a sign and type of both the Virgin Mary and the Church. The consecrated virgin reveals in her person the love of the Church for Christ, the Bridegroom.[131]

[130] *Vita consecrata*, no. 16.

[131] Judith Stegman, "Virginal, Feminine, Spousal Love for Christ," in *An Introduction to the Vocation of Consecrated Virginity Lived in the World: Volume I* (United States Association of Consecrated Virgins, 2012), 100.

The consecrated virgin can, through her virginal integrity, point to the perfect virginity of the Church, who keeps herself pure and completely open to the will of the Bridegroom and who follows no one else but the Bridegroom with a love that is total.[132] In her spousal relationship with the Lord, rooted in her femininity, the consecrated virgin can also reveal that the Church is feminine and spousal in her orientation toward Christ. The woman, united to Christ in spousal love, becomes one with Him in radical receptivity as He is one with the Church, His Bride. The fruit of the union between Christ and the consecrated virgin is souls, and this fruitfulness, seen at the human level, is an image of the spiritual fruitfulness of the Church.

Importantly, the witness of consecrated women in our time can help to heal the vision that some may have of the Church. Though it is a kind of lived witness and not necessarily an explicit one, consecrated virgins, through the holiness of their life (imperfect though we may be), can reveal the virginal beauty of the Church, who gives herself completely to Christ in chaste love. The Church is filled with people who sin (all of us!), but her *nature* is that of a spotless virgin and the lofty call of consecrated virginity, even lived imperfectly, can point to this nature. Just like the Church, who is holy and is becoming holy, consecrated women can also image this in their own lives; brides of Christ are holy by virtue of their Baptism and are being made holy by way of the gratuitous and faithful love of their Bridegroom. Since consecrated virginity is lived in the world, and since the scandals of the Church have especially scandalized those who *are* in the world and whose faith is weaker, there is an enormous potential for healing their skewed vision and revealing the intrinsic holiness of the Church through the witness of the woman's life.

[132] *Sacra virginitas*, no. 30.

Who knows—maybe this is one reason the Lord seems to be calling many women to consecrated virginity in this time!

The Rite of Consecration, in the counsel of the Fathers and in the Tradition of the Church, gives the title "Bride of Christ" to both the Church and the woman, and in this way the consecrated virgin can also be, along with the Church, "a sign of the great mystery of salvation."[133] This mystery is founded in the love of God and witnessed to in a radical way through the woman's complete gift of her whole self in response to receiving Christ's gratuitous love. Through this gift of love, just as the Church extends Christ's saving action in the world, the consecrated virgin also becomes, "in a certain way, a prolongation of his humanity."[134]

The Sign of Consecration "Lived in the World"

There are also some very immediate signs that the consecration gives, even to those who don't have a deep understanding of the Faith, or even for those who are skeptical of it. Mother Mary Francis, a Poor Clare Nun, says to those called to be brides of Christ:

> In our times, false ideas of celibacy are rampant. The great error is to insist that no one can love God, no one could be loved by God so much that he could ask of this person an absolute return of love. You will be there to say, "It *is* possible to love that much. It is possible to be loved by God so much that God can come to me very directly with outstretched arms and say, 'My spouse and no one else's'."[135]

[133] "Homily," in *Rite of Consecration of a Virgin Living in the World*, no. 16.

[134] *Vita consecrata*, no. 76.

[135] Mother Mary Francis, *My Beloved Is Mine and I Am His: Meditations on Brideship for Women Religious* (Cluny Media, 2022), 114.

The witness of one who is joyful and experiences deep fulfillment apart from romantic or sexual encounters or commitments causes deep questions to arise in the hearts of those who long for peace. Even in terms of the sexual appetites themselves, the witness of someone who lives continence with joy and peace presents an almost incomprehensible sign to a world that believes it impossible to experience fulfillment without sexual gratification. Fr. Cantalamessa says this well:

> Since human beings have been unable to use their sexuality to go out of themselves and open up to the love of God and others, but have made sex an idol which they have even called by name (Astarte, Venus ...), it has pleased God to reveal in the Gospel the way of renunciation of the active exercise of sexuality, expressed in continence for the sake of the Kingdom and in perfect chastity.[136]

The witness of celibacy reveals that Jesus is enough; His love is sufficient for the happiness of the human person, and those who reveal this in their vocation cause those they encounter, most especially those who do not know Christ, to question deeply their own ideas around what constitutes fulfillment.

These signs, in varying ways, take on an increased forcefulness in the case of consecrated virgins since the vocation is specifically lived in the world, as Christ's was. This is not to say that religious orders don't imitate the call to follow Christ; they do so in a radical way through the profession of the evangelical counsels. It *is* to say that consecrated virgins, like Christ, live in a kind of intimacy with the culture that they inhabit, unlike religious orders that are characterized by a separation from the world. There are theological

[136] Cantalamessa, *Virginity: A Positive Approach*, 43.

considerations to this, but also very practical ones. Theologically, the consecrated virgin in her person, but also in union with the whole *Ordo Virginum* around the world, becomes all things to all people. The possibility of ways that the Lord may call each woman, rooted in the gifts she has been given on both a natural and a supernatural level, are infinitely variable and make the reach of Christ beautifully diffuse.

Practically, because consecrated virginity is lived in the world, encounters with the people who inhabit the secular spheres that the woman finds herself in should be normative. For a consecrated virgin to live like a diocesan hermit, apart from situations such as health or old age that may be practically similar, is contrary to her vocation. Similarly, if a consecrated virgin is attempting to live the evangelical counsels of poverty and obedience in the same manner that they are lived in religious life, she is living in a way that is contrary to her vocation. For example, the consecrated virgin is required to provide for her own needs in a way that precludes a vow of poverty, and the relationship she has with the diocesan bishop is much different to that of a religious superior. Though not called to be *of* the world in the sense that she takes on the values of secular culture, a consecrated virgin *is* called to be *in* the world.

There is a different way in which the consecrated virgin can reach more souls than in any other vocation. Since she doesn't wear a habit, she is able to bypass, in a sense, some of the baggage that may present an obstacle to building relationships with those who may have been hurt or scandalized by members of the Church. A very specific example of this is the sexual abuse crisis. If some have experienced abuse, or their faith has been severely compromised by the scandals of abuse, it may be that the religious habit of the sister or the clerics of the priest present an obstacle to relationship. In these or similar cases, consecrated virgins can follow the Lord to encounter people in places that other consecrated or ordained persons may not be able to go, and with the freedom characteristic of consecrated life that is not possible for those who are married. She can exercise a spiritual motherhood that is somewhat under the radar.

It's also true that there is a closeness consecrated virgins can have with people that is different from those in other forms of celibate life, by virtue of our *lack* of separation from the context of the world of the every day that is lived by most people. Consecrated virgins set our own schedules, pay our bills, grocery shop, walk our dogs, go on vacations, check the mail, etc. These practical ways of being embedded in normal life are, of course, things that priests and religious also take part in, to varying extents, but most often in a more structured way that dictates much of a daily schedule centered around the horarium of a community or the parish life of a priest.

The Rite of Consecration as a Sacramental

Finally, we can turn toward the consecration itself, which is one of the oldest sacramentals in the Church, to examine what this means. Sacramentals are created through a specific blessing that sets the item or place or person apart. The *Catechism* says, "Among those blessings which are intended for persons—not to be confused with sacramental ordination—are the blessing of the abbot or abbess of a monastery, the consecration of virgins, the rite of religious profession and the blessing of certain ministries of the Church (readers, acolytes, catechists, etc.). The dedication or blessing of a church or an altar, the blessing of holy oils, vessels, and vestments, bells, etc., can be mentioned as examples of blessings that concern objects."[137] Sacramentals are "sacred signs which bear a

[137] CCC, no. 1672.

resemblance to the sacraments. They signify effects, particularly of a spiritual nature, which are obtained through the intercession of the Church. By them men are disposed to receive the chief effect of the sacraments, and various occasions in life are rendered holy."[138]

There are three notable effects of the sacramental aspect of the consecration of virgins living in the world. The first is that the consecration sets consecrated virgins apart as sacred persons (sacramentals). For the woman, she is reminded that something in her is changed, and she is now affirmed as a bride of Christ, and for the community, she takes on the sign values previously identified that are associated with consecrated virginity.

This is an interesting thing to speak about with consecrated virgins, because they will often describe their experience of this differently. For one consecrated virgin I know, she felt that after her consecration, every single cell in her body was new in some way, totally different, changed. For me, I simply felt more *myself*. I also felt a huge relief that, after a long journey of searching and of formation, I was now a bride of Christ, publicly affirmed as such by the Church at the hands of my bishop, and that I can rest in the surety that it is forever. Some women simply experience a profound joy, many (interestingly, and something we'll cover in another chapter) an uptick in suffering, and many other variations on these things. A common thread, though, is that something has *happened*. There is a difference from walking into the church and walking out. Something has somehow changed, however that may be experienced.

The second effect is that, as sacramentals dispose others to receive the sacraments, so the woman living in the graces of her consecration can be a living encounter with grace that inspires

[138] CCC, no. 1667.

others to seek out the graces present in the sacraments. In a sense, sacramentals point toward the sacraments, and the woman herself points toward what it means to live fully in the gifts made available by Christ through His Church. The consecration, as a sacramental, points to the joy of becoming a daughter of God and being conformed to Christ in Baptism, the mercy of God poured out in Reconciliation, the divine indwelling of the Trinity through the gift of the Eucharist, the life of the Holy Spirit given in greater measure in Confirmation, and the healing and sustenance for final perseverance given in the Anointing of the Sick. Even though she is confirmed in a vocation of virginity for the sake of the kingdom, she also points to the Lord's blessing on self-gift and communion seen in the sacraments of Marriage and Ordination.

The final effect is that sacramentals are gifts from God that are intended to be made use of as sources of grace, which means that other members of the Church are, in a sense, entitled to make use of consecrated virgins. This is not in the sense of a utilitarian usage that is opposed to love, but rather in the sense that consecrated virginity is a public vocation in the Church, through which the Church provides motherhood to all her sons and daughters. The members of the Body of Christ—lay, ordained, and consecrated—are invited to find in consecrated virgins a real encounter with the grace of God that stirs a greater desire in the person for the things of God, and for a deeper relationship with the Persons of the Trinity.

In each vocation, there is a form in which our life does not belong to us, but to another. In marriage, the life of a wife belongs primarily to her husband and children, and vice versa. In ordination, the life of the priest or the bishop (and the deacon, to the extent permitted in accord with the need to safeguard family life) belongs to the people entrusted to the spiritual fatherhood of the man. For the deacon, this is generally a parish or a ministry to the poor; for the priest, his parish; and for the bishop, his diocese. In religious life, the man's or woman's life belongs especially to the other members of the community and to those to whom the institute's charism owes its service in accord with its constitutions—though, of course, the spiritual motherhood or fatherhood is made available to whomever the Lord places in front of the person at any given moment. In consecrated virginity, the woman's life belongs in a particular way to the faithful of the diocese she is consecrated in, and especially to the bishop and priests of the diocese, for whom she prays and offers sacrifices.

However, this right to the person is not a one-way street. The gift of self that the consecrated virgin makes for the people of the diocese is a great sacrifice that demands heroic generosity, but there are also innumerable blessings that come in response to such an offering. We would say that in marriage the spouses have a right to each other, and by this we mean a right to the body of the other in the conjugal union, where the communion of their persons is consummated. In this sense, the faithful of the diocese are afforded access to the life of grace in the consecrated virgin, most especially in the form of her prayers, but also in the offering of her gifts to the diocese. There is a communion of persons established between the consecrated virgin and those she pours herself out for, but there is also a reciprocal gift of the other members of the diocese to the consecrated virgin that is entirely necessary. The bishop and priests offer their spiritual fatherhood and care, religious offer a particular form of "bride to bride" friendship, and the laity offer their friendship, prayers and support to consecrated virgins. These gifts of self offered by ordained, consecrated, and laypersons in the diocese are necessary for the consecrated virgin and provide healthy relationships that sustain her in all the different stages of her life, challenge her to live each day in a deeper and deeper relationship with Christ, and affirm her in her belovedness.

A real-life example of this: I recall often the gift of being able to stay from time to time at St. Augustine Seminary in Toronto. When I visit, the priests there are my fathers. They are so clear in their love and their care, from carrying my suitcase, to ensuring I have a pitcher of water in my room, to inquiring about how I am doing. It is a great gift for me, but I think many consecrated women experience the same in acts of priestly generosity, such as when priests rise early to go to a convent to offer Mass for the sisters or take time to offer reflections at a day of recollection. In some sense, it is simply because they are kind men. In a deeper sense, though, they are seeing in the women they are serving the Bride-Church that they are called to lay their lives down for as an *alter Christi*. It is a gift to receive their love, these other Christs after the true Bridegroom, as brides who image the One Bride.

The generosity of a consecrated person must, however, exist within the limits imposed by the reality of our human condition. We have a positive precept to care for our physical health, and it's also important to know what it means to balance prudently the demands of our life, which include our responsibility to our relationship with God, respecting the limitations naturally existing in each of us in terms of capacities (physical, emotional, mental), and the call to pour ourselves out in love without counting the cost. This can be a difficult balance to juggle at times. Dom Dysmas de Lassus has a beautiful way of looking at the impetus for generous love:

> St. Bernard says, "How much love should we offer to God? A measureless amount!" On the other hand, there are limits to our human nature, to our physical strength, to

our health, to our psychological makeup, and it is here that the risks are to be found: love has no limits—no one will ever love too much—but the various tools designed to help our love blossom do have limits, and if we go beyond these, then these very tools may end up leading to death rather than life. From these remarks a first important conclusion can be drawn: love has no limits because it is divine, but expressions of love do have limits because they are human.... Our love for God can be expressed by various types of sacrifices—fasting, for example. But a religious will never be able to intensify his fasting so that it keeps pace with his growing love for God, since here, too, he will run into two constraints: the number of days in the week, and his body's need for food. So while it is always possible for our love to increase, the same is not true of the ways we show our love. These will always fall short, and the one who loves will always feel some regret about that, but this will diminish over time, since the deeper the love grows, the easier it becomes to sum it up in a few simple words, "I love you, and I am certain of your love, and that is enough for me."[139]

Practical Applications: "in the World" but Not "of the World"

The reality of a vocation specifically named "in the world" necessitates having a full awareness of what this means before receiving the consecration. Living "in the world" entails a closeness to the

[139] Dom Dysmas de Lassus, *Abuses in the Religious Life and the Path to Healing* (Sophia Institute Press, 2023), 24–25.

world of sin and, though "where sin increased, grace increased all the more" (Rom. 5:20), it is essential to have an awareness of some of the pitfalls, such as loneliness, lack of immediate accountability, lack of assured financial security, the weight of responsibility for all practical tasks that would otherwise be shared with a spouse or community (e.g. keeping up a house, paying bills and managing finances, etc.), and susceptibility to infection by the values of the secular culture. We can't underestimate the power of the enemy to attack this vocation because of its powerful witness embedded in the world. However, it is precisely this being embedded in the world without being imbued with worldliness that causes people to pause and to question how this is possible and, ultimately, who makes it possible. It is essential that any woman who receives the consecration to the life of virginity lived in the world have a deep self-knowledge and a deep humility and distrust of her own capacities so that she is constantly depending on the Lord to sustain her vocation.

Though, of course, we don't have a certainty of what will happen in the future, entry into this vocation necessitates that the woman being able to come to a prudent judgment of whether the gifts and capacities she has for self-discipline and self-motivation are developed enough to receive the consecration responsibly. It's certainly not a matter of perfection; otherwise, there would be no consecrated virgins anywhere. Rather, it is a matter of allowing the Lord to show us, using all the indications at His disposal, including our natural capacities, where He is calling us to be.

It's important to note in this regard that consecrated virginity is a public vocation in the Church. There has sometimes been an emphasis on the hidden aspect of consecrated virginity, as though it were something to be purposefully concealed in one's life. It is very true that it is a hidden vocation in many respects—the woman does not wear a habit, or any other visible sign apart from the ring that she receives at her consecration, and there is certainly a great benefit to being able to infiltrate the world in a way that is under the radar and not possible for other consecrated persons (especially those who wear the habit).

Though prudence may occasionally dictate, depending on the profession and the colleagues one has, that disclosing a vocation of consecrated virginity could be detrimental to relationships or job security, in most cases this is not necessary. The hiddenness of the vocation is tied to the ordinariness of the life of the woman, and not by an intentional hiding of her vocation. On the contrary, the rite itself calls for reasonable notice to be given to the local faith community, such that they can attend the consecration Mass. The faithful are invited to know the consecrated virgins of the diocese so that they may ask for prayers or benefit from the spiritual motherhood of the woman. Having a public vocation means, as we have said, that the faithful have a certain right to you—to your love, and to your time, in accord with reason and ability. This is an important point to emphasize because the witness and value of the sign of virginity is *meant* to be seen so that its presence can impact the beholder.

Questions and Scriptures for Reflections

1. How is the Lord showing me my own capacity to express the sign values of consecrated virginity?

2. How do I feel about the public nature of the vocation and the "right" the faithful have to my love? What limits of my human nature do I experience in my capacity to express love, and how might I pay attention to these so that they do not end up becoming tools "leading to death rather than life"?

3. How do I experience life-giving love from those in other vocations in my diocese?

4. How do I understand the public and hidden natures of consecrated virginity?

Isaiah 65:17–25
Matthew 10:34–39
Matthew 13:24–30
Romans 5:6–21
1 John 3:11–18

6

Brideship and Spousal Love

In the consecrated life, particular importance attaches to the spousal meaning, which recalls the Church's duty to be completely and exclusively devoted to her Spouse, from whom she receives every good thing. This spousal dimension, which is part of all consecrated life, has a particular meaning for women, who find therein their feminine identity and as it were discover the special genius of their relationship with the Lord.[140]

The Fundamentally Spousal Nature of Consecrated Virginity

The spousal nature of the relationship of the consecrated virgin with the Lord is written into the whole of the vocation, right from the study of its origins to the woman's initial discernment and testing of a vocation through to the Mass of consecration. Within the Rite of Consecration itself, we see many bridal elements, including the presentation of the insignia of the veil and the ring, along with the admonition to "Keep unstained your

[140] *Vita consecrata*, no. 34.

fidelity to your Bridegroom."[141] It is traditional for a consecrated virgin to wear a wedding dress for the Mass, and the entire liturgy contains references to spousal love and the nuptial relationship of the consecrated virgin with Christ.

In the homily for the consecration, it is said that the woman receives a new title—I shall call you by a new name pronounced by the mouth of the Lord (see Isa. 62:2)—and that is "bride of Christ."[142] It is along the lines of names and titles given by God to many over the course of history to signify a radical change in their person. Peter was given a new name as God instituted the Petrine office and entrusted to him the keys of the kingdom forever. Abram and Sarai were called Abraham and Sarah as they were to be the parents of all nations. Many religious take a new name to signify the new reality that is taking place. It isn't a temporary or an earthly change—it is a change forever, because when God speaks a word, both directly in historical contexts and indirectly through the authority of the Church in current ones, He makes a reality of what is being spoken. As in the Mass, the words "This *is* my body" bring into being what they state; so the title "bride of Christ" spoken in the consecration in the name of the Church makes the woman so. She is now in reality the bride of the Bridegroom forever. The woman now "*eloquently expresses her [the Church's] inmost nature as 'Bride'*."[143]

The spousal meaning of consecrated virginity is rooted in the fundamental spousal meaning of the body. To refresh us, the spousal meaning of the body is the incarnated ability of human

[141] "Presentation of the Insignia," in *Rite of Consecration of a Virgin Living in the World*, nos. 25–27.

[142] "Homily," in *Rite of Consecration of a Virgin Living in the World*, no. 16.

[143] *Vita consecrata*, no. 105.

persons to exist in a dynamism of gift and, in doing so, to live fully the meaning of their own existence. The spousal meaning of the virginal body lies in its capacity to enter into communion with Christ through mutual self-gift between the consecrated virgin and Christ, in such a way that this nuptial love transmits itself into the world as a gift. In other words, "Man . . . cannot fully find himself except through a sincere gift of himself,"[144] and the woman finds in her nuptial relationship with Christ that she was created for infinite love and, living in the power of this discovery, her union with Him sanctifies the woman and becomes an efficacious sign of love for the world. She becomes a sign of what every soul is called to—marriage with the divine—but the sign of her nuptial union also transmits into the world the life-giving love of Christ.

To frame all that is part of the spousal union between Christ and the consecrated virgin is to be reminded that, "We love because he first loved us" (1 John 4:19). Receiving the invitation to belong to Christ as one mystically betrothed to Him depends entirely on His first action of sacrificial self-offering; it is this self-offering that invites the response of love and establishes the foundation of spousal love between Christ and the consecrated virgin.

The Scent of the Bride

Christopher West brings together several interesting points when discussing the love of the Bridegroom for the bride that can assist us in appreciating the nature of Christ's love for His bride.[145] In

[144] *Gaudium et spes*, no. 24.

[145] See Christopher West, "Holy Week, The Week of the Bridegroom," posted March 29, 2021, Theology of the Body Institute, YouTube, https://www.youtube.com/watch?v=HCpiXOIGVeA.

the middle of the Song of Songs, which itself is at the centre of the Bible, stand the verses:

> You have ravished my heart, my sister, my bride; you have ravished my heart with one glance of your eyes, with one bead of your necklace. How beautiful is your love, my sister, my bride, How much better is your love than wine, and the fragrance of your perfumes than any spice! Your lips drip honey, my bride, honey and milk are under your tongue; And the fragrance of your garments is like the fragrance of Lebanon. A garden enclosed, my sister, my bride, a garden enclosed, a fountain sealed! Your branches are a grove of pomegranates, with fruits of choicest yield: Henna with spikenard, spikenard and saffron, Sweet cane and cinnamon, with all kinds of frankincense; myrrh and aloes, with all the finest spices; A garden fountain, a well of living water, streams flowing from Lebanon. Awake, north wind! Come, south wind! Blow upon my garden that its perfumes may spread abroad. (Song of Songs 4:9–16, NABRE)

Within this passage is a double reference to spikenard, which is an extremely pungent and costly perfume. A few drops would suffice to retain the scent strongly, so much so that even washing could not always remove the scent.

In Song of Songs, the fragrance of spikenard is explicitly associated with the presence and love of the bride. It also reveals the bridegroom's overflowing desire for the bride and his ability to associate her presence simply by the scents that accompany her person. The bride is "a garden enclosed, a fountain sealed"; she is solely given to her bridegroom and her love is for him alone. He is enraptured by her and captivated by her beauty. The love between the bride and bridegroom of the Song of Songs is nuptial to its core.

Many saints and Fathers of the Church, such as Gregory the Great, who have written expositions on the Song of Songs overwhelmingly see its nuptial imagery as an allegory for the relationship between God and His people or God and the soul.[146] It can, in this way, be informed by the passage in Ephesians 5:22–23, which describes the spousal relationship between Christ and the Church that is imaged by marital love. In this light, we can see the depths of Christ's sacrifice on the Cross; He is giving His very life for the Bride by whom He is captivated.

Taking place six days before the Passover, we read this in the Scriptures:

> Six days before the Passover, Jesus came to Bethany, where Lazarus lived, whom Jesus had raised from the dead. Here a dinner was given in Jesus' honor. Martha served, while Lazarus was among those reclining at the table with him. Then Mary took about a pint of pure nard [spikenard], an expensive perfume; she poured it on Jesus' feet and wiped his feet with her hair. And the house was filled with the fragrance of the perfume. But one of his disciples, Judas Iscariot, who was later to betray him, objected, "Why wasn't this perfume sold and the money given to the poor? It was worth a year's wages." He did not say this because he cared about the poor but because he was a thief; as keeper of the money bag, he used to help himself to what was put into it. "Leave her alone," Jesus replied. "It was intended that she should save this perfume for the day of my burial. You will

[146] Gregory the Great, "An Exposition on the Song of Songs," Lectio Divina, accessed August 24, 2024, https://www.lectio-divina.org/images/patristics/Commentary%20on%20the%20Song%20of%20Songs%20by% 20Gregory%20the%20Great.pdf.

always have the poor among you, but you will not always have me (John 12:1–8).

We can immediately notice the presence of spikenard in the passage. Remembering how pungent the scent is, we can imagine the smell when, not a few drops but a whole pint, is used to anoint the feet of Jesus. The Scripture itself says that the entire house was "filled with the odour." Additionally, Mary's hair, used to dry the feet of Christ, was also filled with the scent.

Mary symbolizes the bride of Song of Songs in this passage, who "opens her garden," characterized by the scent of the spikenard, to the bridegroom; since the Song of Songs is an allegory for the nuptial relationship between Christ and His Church, she also symbolizes the Church, who opens up to pour the fragrance of Herself over Christ as an anointing of love.

During the rest of Passion week, into the Passover meal, through to the Passion and death of Christ, and even into His resurrection, Christ carried the scent of the bride. He carried with Him the scent of the one for whom He was giving His life as a constant impetus of love. His bride was never anywhere but before His eyes at every moment, and the smell of her whom He loves permeated and carried Him through His sacrificial offering.

Spousal Celibacy as a True Marriage in the Spiritual Order

The only sufficient response to this love of the Bridegroom by one who is called to be His spouse echoes the mother of Jesus at the Annunciation: "May it be done to me according to your word" (Luke 1:38, NABRE). It is, simply put, to give Him everything—to give Him our whole selves without reserve, trusting that He wants all of it. Truly, a spousal relationship with Christ, though informed by our understanding of human marriage, is a place of mystery:

> Instead of a marriage between equals this holy union is between a creature and her Creator. The finite creation enveloped by infinite love. There is a deeper mutual self-giving as God may freely communicate Himself to the attentive soul. The bride in turn is perfectly known and comprehended by her Beloved. Thus a higher more perfect union is achieved. Virginity itself becomes the enduring and radiant sign of our eternal marriage with the Lamb.[147]

Though the spousal union of the consecrated virgin with Christ does not occur in the natural order proper to human marriage, it lives out, even now, what the spousal embrace signifies. However, some care is necessary in describing the nature of this union. For example, there are many Ancient Near East creation stories that depict sexual or marital relationships between the gods and human beings.[148] This is not at all what is signified in the nuptial relationship of the consecrated virgin and Christ, as if the relationship could be somehow anthropomorphized.

Ecclesiae Sponsae Imago uses two interesting terms when discussing the spousal nature of consecrated virginity: theogamic and theologal. Theogamic refers to what consecrated virginity is *not*: marriage with the divinity (including sexual elements proper to human marriage). Theologal refers to what consecrated virginity

[147] Diane Farr, "The Essence of the Consecrated Virgin's Mystical Espousal to Christ," *The Lamp* (newsletter), September 2007, 3.

[148] Joshua J. Mark, "Enuma Elish: The Babylonian Epic of Creation," *World History Encyclopedia*, May 4, 2018, https://www.world history.org/article/225/enuma-elish--the-babylonian-epic-of-creation--fu/.

is: a mystical spousal union meant to be understood through a theological lens that properly takes into account the nature of the relationship between the consecrated virgin and Christ.[149] The spousal reality of consecrated virginity is not something where marriage is, in a sense, pulled down to the physical reality of sexuality in human marriage, but rather where the consecrated virgin is drawn up into the eternal realities that human marriage signifies.

The Mystical Marriage Between Christ and the Consecrated Virgin

The relationship between the consecrated virgin and Christ *is* a very real marriage, and its theologal meaning is itself a nuptial reality:

> Christian virginity is an experience of spousal union, intimate, exclusive and indissoluble, with the divine bridegroom, who has given himself to humanity without reserve and forever.... For consecrated virginity the spousal experience is one of transcendence and the surprising humility of God. Consecration takes place through the pact of covenant and fidelity that unites the virgin to the Lord in a mystical marriage, deepening and enlarging her sharing in his mind and her conformation to his desire to love.[150]

[149] *Ecclesiae Sponsae Imago,* no. 17. The term theologal is used in *Ecclesiae Sponsae Imago,* but it seems the word either does not exist in the English language or is not well defined. I've attempted here to offer a definition in accord with what the text seems to be conveying, but it is likely that the understanding of the terms theogamic and theologal will be further developed in the future.

[150] *Ecclesiae Sponsae Imago,* no. 24.

Spousal union with Christ thus takes place in the order of the Spirit. Consecrated virgins are "betrothed mystically to Christ, the Son of God, and are dedicated to the service of the Church."[151]

We can look to the nature of the spousal relationship in human marriage, the sign of the eternal realities of mystical marriage, to give other insights into the spousal relationship between Christ and the consecrated virgin. Human spouses have particular roles of reception and donation in sexual union, dictated by their very bodies (though this does not negate the reality of intentional self-gift each brings to the sexual act). There is a dynamism and communion between the spouses that is revealed in and through their bodies which reveals something important. The nature of this intercommunion is what Cardinal Angelo Scola calls asymmetrical reciprocity: the ability of Adam and Eve to exist in a communion of persons and to fulfill the spousal meaning revealed through their bodies can occur precisely because their bodies share a common nature *and* a complementary differentiation.[152]

In previous chapters, we have seen that the spousal meaning of the body, meaning the call for the human person to enter into a communion of self-gift with another, is not restricted to those who are married. Thus, the asymmetrical reciprocity seen in the union of spouses also makes possible communion in other orders of human relationships. This asymmetrical reciprocity extends, in the realm of the Spirit, to the relationship between Christ, God Incarnate, and the consecrated virgin, who is human yet willed by Christ to be united to Him.

151 CCC, no. 923.

152 Angelo Cardinal Scola, *The Nuptial Mystery* (Michigan: William B. Eerdmans Publishing Company, 2005), 645.

Sexuality is part of the human person, and simply because the nuptial relationship between Christ and the consecrated virgin is mystical in nature does not mean that sexuality is put aside or repressed. In other words, women respond to God *as women*. Consecrated women are not asexual; our sexuality, our womanhood, is an important aspect of *how* we relate to God. Hearkening back to the asymmetrical reciprocity of the sexual union of spouses, there is a receptivity (not passive, but actively engaging in self-gift), that the woman engages in. This receptivity is foundational in the relationship between Christ and the consecrated virgin and is an intentional posture that we can (and need to!) develop more and more over time.

An essential virtue for this is faith—because our Spouse is very real, but not enfleshed in the way that a human spouse is. We are invited to express our receptivity through our faith in Christ and in what He has revealed to us. As faith is a virtue, we need to ask continually for this gift. Part of our growth in receptivity is simply asking for an increase in faith to allow us to believe more deeply in the things that have been shown to us—that some are called to consecrated life and that Christ has called us in particular, that we are truly made His Bride in the consecration, and that He longs to be united more and more closely with us, despite our brokenness and lack of receptivity in various areas.

We've also looked at Matthew 19:22, which speaks of the union between man and woman as one flesh. St. Paul expounds on this union in Ephesians 5:22–33, where he characterizes the relationship between Christ and the Church as nuptial. From this, we can understand the Mass to be a place of union, both between Christ and His Church and between Christ and each worshipper, where both parties engage in reciprocal self-gift.

In earthly marriage, the nuptial union of the spouses is characterized by complete, reciprocal self-gift, and is a sign of the union each soul is called to have with God in eternal life. For the consecrated virgin, who touches this union here and now through her fundamentally spousal union with Christ, the Eucharist takes on special significance. During the Mass, the altar is the place of mystical, marital union between the consecrated virgin and Christ because there He gives us His body, which we receive; and receiving Him, we give our whole selves back to Him. Though reciprocal self-gift in and through the Eucharist is something that all the baptized are called to, the already-spousal union of Christ and the consecrated virgin touches the nuptial reality of eternal life intimately.

In the sacrament of marriage, the mutual gaze of spouses on their respective masculinity and femininity speaks to them of the spousal meaning of their bodies and constitutes a special intimacy shared only between the two. In times of eucharistic adoration, we can find a similar intimacy of spouses who gaze at each other with unveiled eyes, and who see in each other the beauty of the self-gift that makes their communion possible. It is true that consecrated virgins must

> place the Eucharist at the centre of their existence. It is the sacrament of the spousal covenant from which flows the grace of their consecration.... They express the love of the Church as Bride for the Eucharist also in the prayer of adoration of the Eucharistic Body of the Lord, and from him they draw effective charity towards the members of his mystical Body."[153]

Practical Applications: The Realities of Spousal Union with the Divine

St. Gregory of Nyssa indicated some distinguishing factors about what it means to be a bride of Christ, in particular:

[153] *Ecclesiae Sponsae Imago*, no. 32.

> How they congratulate those who have chosen from the first the virgin life, and have not had to learn by experience about the better way, that virginity is fortified against all these ills, that it has no orphan state, no widowhood to mourn; it is always in the presence of the undying Bridegroom; it has the offspring of devotion always to rejoice in; it sees continually a home that is truly its own, furnished with every treasure because the Master always dwells there; in this case death does not bring separation, but union with Him Who is longed for.[154]

John Paul II says, in reference to the imagery laid out in Ephesians regarding marriage as a sign of the relationship between Christ and the Church, "The Bridegroom is the one who loves. The Bride is loved: *it is she who receives love, in order to love in return.*"[155] This is the experience of the consecrated virgin in relation to Christ.

The spousal reality of consecrated virginity also has profound effects on the woman and is, in a sense, educative to her regarding her own identity:

> By freely choosing virginity, women confirm themselves as persons, as beings whom the Creator from the beginning has willed for their own sake. At the same time they realize the personal value of their own femininity by becoming "a sincere gift" for God who has revealed himself in Christ, a gift for Christ, the Redeemer of humanity and the Spouse of souls: a "spousal" gift. *One cannot correctly understand*

[154] St. Gregory of Nyssa, *On Virginity*, chap. 3.

[155] *Mulieris dignitatem*, no. 29.

> *virginity*—a woman's consecration in virginity—*without referring to spousal love.* It is through this kind of love that a person becomes a gift for the other.[156]

It also demands great love because of *Who* is being loved, which is a great gift for the woman because it calls her deeply into the meaning of her existence, which is to love. St. Augustine says, "Love with all your hearts Him Who is the most beautiful of the sons of men: you are free, your hearts are not fettered by conjugal bonds.... If, then, you would owe your husbands great love, how great is the love you owe Him because of Whom you have willed to have not husbands? Let Him Who was fastened to the cross be securely fastened to your hearts."[157] John Paul II says this another way: "It is a characteristic feature of the human heart to accept even difficult demands in the name of love, for an ideal, and above all *in the name of love for a person* (love is, in fact, oriented by its very nature toward the person)."[158]

As a spouse of Christ, the Praenotanda (the introductory comments from the Rite of Consecration of a Virgin Living in the World) indicates that the woman does the works of her spouse—works of penance and mercy, in apostolic activity, and in prayer. It makes me recall two good friends of mine who, when they got married, discerned together the mission by which their marriage would be guided. In this way, they can focus the things they include in their family life and the activities they take on, according to the sense of this mission that they feel the Lord has entrusted to them, in order to remain faithful to and focused on the mission. For us, the mission is even clearer because our Spouse is perfect, which means our spousal mission *is* His mission. We are called to

156 Ibid., no. 20.

157 St. Augustine, *De Sancta Virginitate*, cc. 54–55; PL XL, 428.

158 John Paul II, *Man and Woman He Created Them*, no. 80.1.

be one with Christ and to have one will that is united in carrying out the will of the Father, which is what Jesus is always concerned most about.

However, the reality is that this vocation is lived by human women with all their sinfulness and woundedness. It's also lived without the closeness of a religious community to provide regular guidance. The relationship with the bishop and other consecrated virgins or consecrated women and the support of a spiritual director are essential, but they are not daily meetings. There are not necessarily people around you to rouse you from bed if you are missing your prayer time! Because of the convergence of these two points, it can be a temptation to compare our lives as consecrated virgins to those of other consecrated virgins or religious sisters and to find ourselves coming up short.

Not too long after my consecration, a friend who had joined a religious order was interviewed on a podcast, and I remember listening and really being struck by how beautiful she was in her vocation, and by how clear it was that she was living in her spousal identity. My next thought was one of comparison: "Lord, I should be more like her; I feel like I'm failing you as a spouse." It felt like a lot of insecurity was coming up all at once. Was I praying as much as a spouse of Christ should be praying? Was I cutting secular influences out of my life enough to prevent God being drowned out? Was I living my days as I should be? Why did life after consecration feel so much like life before it?

It wasn't long before the Lord provided the beautiful assurance that He knows the desires of my heart and honors them. There is a beautiful prayer in a book called *The Cloud of Unknowing* that says:

> O God, all hearts are open to you.
> You perceive my desire.

> Nothing is hidden from you.
> Purify the thoughts of my heart
> with the gift of your Spirit,
> that I may love you with a perfect love
> and give you the praise you deserve. Amen.[159]

Other translations of the book give the second line as, "Upon whom desire is eloquent." It doesn't mean that our actions are not important, because they are, but Jesus very aptly reminded me that He sees the desire of my heart to love Him "with a perfect love," and that to be frustrated by my limitations is both prideful and lacking trust in the perfection of *His* love, which is not dependent on anything apart from my *yes* to receive it.

We come into this spousal relationship with Christ not because of any merit on our part, but simply because He has chosen us. It can be a temptation to feel, because of the dissonance between the love that we *desire* to give the Lord and love that we are *able* to give Him, that we are not enough for Him. We don't need to fear this reality, though, because He doesn't hold our weaknesses and limitations against us. As John Paul II said at World Youth Day in Toronto, "We are not the sum of our weaknesses and failures; we are the sum of the Father's love for us and our real capacity to become the image of his Son."[160] Truly, it *is* the living of the vocation—the coming close to His heart as His spouse—that conforms us to Him over time and brings about our holiness and our greater capacity to love as we desire.

[159] Author unknown, *The Cloud of Unknowing*, ed. Bernard Bangley (Paraclete Press, 2006), 18.

[160] John Paul II, 17th World Youth Day Homily, July 28, 2002, no. 5, https://www.vatican.va/content/john-paul-ii/en/homilies/2002/documents/hf_jp-ii_hom_20020728_xvii-wyd.html.

Questions and Scriptures for Reflection

1. What elements of the spousal nature of consecrated virginity resonate with you?

2. What strikes you about Jesus carrying "the scent of the Bride" through His Passion and Resurrection?

3. How would you describe the difference between "theologal" and "theogamic"?

4. How have you experienced your own limitations with regard to loving Christ?

Song of Songs 4:9–16
Isaiah 62:1–5
Luke 1:26–38
John 12:1–8

7

Marian Elements of Consecrated Virginity

"Imitate the Mother of God; desire to be called and to be handmaids of the Lord" (Rite of Consecration to a Life of Virginity for Women Living in the World *[*RCV*], n. 17). The Order of Virgins is a special expression of consecrated life that blossomed anew in the Church after the Second Vatican Council (cf. Post-Synodal Apostolic Exhortation* Vita Consecrata, *n. 7). Its roots, however, are ancient; they date back to the dawn of apostolic times when, with unheard of daring, certain women began to open their hearts to the desire for consecrated virginity, in other words, to the desire to give the whole of their being to God, which had had its first extraordinary fulfilment in the Virgin of Nazareth and her "yes". In the thought of the Fathers Mary was the prototype of* Christian *virgins and their perception highlighted the newness of this new state of life, to which a free choice of love gave access.*[161]

[161] Benedict XVI, Address to the Participants in the International Congress-Pilgrimage of the Ordo Virginum, May 15, 2008, https://www.vatican.va/content/benedict-xvi/en/speeches/2008/may/documents/hf_ben-xvi_spe_20080515_ordo-virginum.html.

Mary's Reception of the Gift of Virginity

In the earlier years after my reversion to Catholicism, when I found out about the consecration to Jesus through Our Lady, it was the much loved *33 Days to Morning Glory* that I read in preparation. I remember a year later it came time to renew my consecration and I thought with some surprise, "Hmmm, I don't know that Mary has been that present in my life this year." Immediately, I felt the Lord take me through major things that had happened in the year and telling me that it had been Mary who arranged them all because I belong in a special way to her through the consecration. I was immediately filled with both a sadness that I doubted her love for me and her presence in my life, as well as a deep gratitude for the ways she had shown me her love and the love of her Son for me, even when it went unacknowledged.

I once heard an analogy that Mary is like the moon; the moon has no light of its own, but it reflects the light of the sun so beautifully that it appears as though it possesses its own light. Mary is, in some ways, like this, because all the good that we are and possess is a reflection of God, in whose image and likeness we were created. Mary is the most perfect creature, and therefore her ability to reveal God's light and love is unmatched. Mary possesses this light in a way unique to all others (save Jesus Himself, who is both God and Man) because there is nothing in her that diminishes the reflection of God in her being.

As consecrated virgins, the Ever-Virgin Mary is our predecessor in virginity and the one from whom Christian virginity springs. It is the first instance of God's unmistakeable blessing on virginity that is offered for the kingdom of God. Mary's offering of virginity to God for the sake of His plan is responded to with His immense generosity: God creates a dwelling for Himself in the womb of the Virgin Mother and sanctifies every woman thereafter who embraces the gift of virginity for the sake of the kingdom. Mary was the first consecrated virgin, who "lived what Scripture says we will all live through eternity—not in human married love, but in spousal union and love with God Himself."[162] It is this great mystery that the consecrated virgin is living in her person.

Consecrated virgins find the meaning of their own virginity within the meaning of Mary's virginity. The Fathers of the Church refer to Jesus as the "Arch-Virgin (Archiparthenos)" and Mary as the "Ever-Virgin (Aiparthenos)."[163] Christ is the one who *is* virgin by nature—recall that we spoke previously of the virgin nature of the Trinity—but Mary is and remains a virgin by choice in the word of her *fiat* and "Christian virginity [was] born of the *yes* of Mary to the Annunciation of the Lord." [164] For "those to whom it has been given (Matt. 19:11)" an embrace of consecrated virginity is an echo of the *fiat* of Our Lady and a continuation of her radical openness that made possible the saving work of Christ.

We can also see through Mary the gratuitousness of God toward those who embrace the gift of virginity: "Mary did not 'find favor with God' because she was a virgin; she was a virgin because she had found favor with God, and she was chosen so that through her the beginnings of the Kingdom on earth would be uncontaminated."[165] For God to have favored Mary because of her virginity would have been utilitarian; rather, she is infinitely loved by God and given the gift of virginity from the moment of her conception. She is given the gift of virginity in a way that is unmerited—this is clear *because* it is present in her from birth, meaning that there is no

[162] Stegman, "Consecrated Virginity," 24.

[163] Cantalamessa, *Virginity: A Positive Approach*, 86.

[164] Ratzinger, "Gift in the Church."

[165] Cantalamessa, *Virginity: A Positive Approach*, 89.

possibility that her works resulted in such a gift. The same is true for us, in that God does not give us this gift, or value this gift in us, because of anything that we have done to merit it or anything we will do through it. He gives the gift not to use us in a utilitarian sense, but so that we might use it and live in the divine gift of His love in a way that brings happiness and joy through holiness.

Eve, a "Type" of Mary

Mary is also a "type," in the form of scriptural interpretation called typology. Typology "discerns in God's works of the Old Covenant prefigurations of what he accomplished in the fullness of time in the person of his incarnate Son."[166] One example of this is the Old Testament figure of Melchizedek, a priest who offers sacrifice, in that Melchizedek prefigures the priesthood of Christ, who is the definitive priest and the one from whom all priests take their priesthood. Adam (the first man) is a "type" of Christ, who is called the New or Second Adam and who comes to make straight all that was put astray by the sin of the first Adam.

Church Tradition calls Mary the New or Second Eve, whose fiat responds with a resounding *yes* to the catastrophic *no* of the first Eve. Mary, as the New Eve, becomes the mother of all who will be reborn in Baptism and live in Christ, just as the first Eve was called the mother of all the living. Also linking the New Eve with the first Eve, Jesus refers to Mary as "woman" at the wedding feast of Cana, on the occasion of the first public manifestation of His saving mission. This beginning of His mission comes as the divine answer to the first one who was called "woman," Eve, through whom sin entered the world. "From this vantage point the two

[166] CCC, no. 128.

female figures, *Eve* and *Mary*, are joined under the *name of woman*. The words of the Protoevangelium [the first announcement of the coming of Christ, Genesis 3:15], re-read in the light of the New Testament, express well the mission of woman in the Redeemer's salvific struggle against the author of evil in human history."[167]

John Paul II points out something very important that resides in this Eve-Mary analogy. In it, Mary is seen as

> the full revelation of all that is included in the biblical word "woman": a revelation commensurate with the mystery of the Redemption. *Mary* means, in a sense, a going beyond the limit spoken of in the Book of Genesis (3:16) and a return to that "beginning" in which one finds the "woman" as she was intended to be in *creation*, and therefore in the eternal mind of God: in the bosom of the Most Holy Trinity. Mary is "the new beginning" of the *dignity and vocation of women*, of each and every woman.[168]

Mary reveals the perfection of womanhood, and of all that is feminine.[169]

God also gives new dignity to the state of virginity through Mary. We can recall from our study of the history of consecrated virginity that Judaism considered perpetual virginity to be a cause for shame. God chose in Mary to link the presence of perpetual virginity to a meaning not of shame, but of the fullness and fulfillment of God's covenant with His people. Mary's perpetual virginity, linked to the birth of Christ who is the fulfillment of all things, makes virginity, consecrated to God, a sign of salvation:

[167] *Mulieris dignitatem*, no. 11.
[168] Ibid.
[169] Ibid., no. 5.

> The infancy Gospels of Matthew (1:18–25) and above all of Luke (1:26–38) present the newness of the virginity (*carnis et cordis*) [of the flesh and of the heart] of the mother of Jesus, a visible sign of the invisible incarnation of the Son of God and a spousal expression of the covenant with God, to which all believers are called.[170]

Reconciling Contrary Definitions in and through Mary

When I first came back to a full practice of the Faith, there were many times when I thought I was an outlier in terms of traits that are often associated with femininity, such as meekness or gentleness (though I've since learned that these descriptions are wider than the image they typically convey). I, in some sense, reconciled myself with only being a half-hearted woman because of the characteristics that I lacked and that I thought reflected Mary's womanhood. However, it was Mary herself who course-corrected me.

While on a yearly retreat, I was asked to spend an imaginative prayer experience with Mary, Joseph, and the Baby Jesus after His birth. It wasn't to be a time that was based on a scriptural passage, but rather just simply a time to *be* with them all. During my time of prayer, after making sure she was okay, Joseph left to find some clean water and food. Mary, passing Jesus to me so that I could hold Him, went about getting herself clean and settled and preparing the things that Jesus would need. As she was cleaning and we were talking, the things I noticed about her were the very things I had thought betrayed authentic femininity. She was strong, determined, full of vigor, powerful in spirit, confident, and adventurous in

[170] *Ecclesiae Sponsae Imago*, no. 15.

addition to being authentically humble and gentle, among many other things. Mary was showing me that I have a place in the fullest definition of what it means to be a woman, and that each woman has the ability to reveal femininity in various, non-competing ways.

Every woman, in this way, can find what it means to be a woman in the fullness of its reality that is found in the Blessed Virgin. The definitions that relate to various aspects of womanhood take on new and reconciled relationships in the person of Mary. She is not gentle in a way that is opposed to strength, or pious in a way that is opposed to industriousness. She does not sacrifice anything of the real meanings inherent to the feminine genius to fit into caricatures.

Her virginity itself, considering the conception of Christ by the *overshadowing* of the Holy Spirit, is a sign of the intervention of God and of His blessing, which elevates the meaning of virginity into the realm of fruitfulness, without sacrificing purity and perfect celibate chastity. Just as God tied meanings of suffering and redemption together in the Person of Christ, His work in Mary links the previously contrary realities of virginity, brideship, and motherhood.

Mary is described in the Eastern tradition as "the Unwedded Bride," because she is unwedded in the human sense of the word but wedded in the order of the Spirit. This is what we hear in the Byzantine hymn, "Rejoice, O Unwedded Bride," and it is also what consecrated virgins participate in.[171] Those who are consecrated can becomes spouses and mothers in the realm of the Spirit through Mary's entry into these mutually exclusive realities and their reconciliation within her person.

[171] See Nectarios of Aegina, performed by Petros Gaitanos, "Greek Byzantine orthodox chant: Agni Parthene," posted January 22, 2019, by Adoration of the Cross, YouTube, https://www.youtube.com/watch?v=i-3h9TQ312c.

Mary, Spouse of the Holy Spirit

Who, then, is Mary's Spouse? The Holy Spirit. It is the Holy Spirit who overshadows Mary in order that she might conceive the Savior in her womb; and her spousal relationship with the Holy Spirit and the effects of this relationship, fruitfulness, are now linked together in the womb of the Virgin and form the solid foundation on which these two realities might also be linked in the persons of virgins for the sake of the kingdom. As quoted by Fr. Manteau-Bonamy, St. Maximilian Kolbe writes:

> What sort of union is this? It is above all an interior union, a union of her essence with the "essence" of the Holy Spirit. The Holy Spirit dwells in her, lives in her. This was true from the first instance of her existence.... Among creatures made in God's image the union brought about by married love is the most intimate of all (cf. Mt. 19:6). In a much more precise, more interior, more essential manner, the Holy Spirit lives in the soul of the Immaculata, in the depths of her very being. He makes her fruitful, from the very first instant of her existence, all during her life, and for all eternity.[172]

Those women who live celibacy for the kingdom of Heaven also have a spousal relationship with the Holy Spirit, whose action in and through us produces fruit in the realm of spiritual motherhood. Mary's example in the fullness of her *fiat* and the gift of her openness to the Holy Spirit lay before us a model of docility. To be docile to the Holy Spirit is to be leadable. To be

[172] H. M. Manteau-Bonamy, O.P., *Immaculate Conception and the Holy Spirit*, trans. Richard Arnandez, F.S.C. (Franciscan Marytown Press, 1977), 2.

led, we need to know how to listen. In both elements, the Blessed Mother shows us the path. To listen, we follow her example as she pondered these things in her heart (Luke 2:19), and we spend time in prayer and silence to come to know the voice of the Holy Spirit in our hearts.

For Mary, there was no disconnect, delay, or even consideration between listening to the Spirit and carrying out the will of God. Such are the effects of her preservation from Original Sin. For us, the effects of Original Sin *do* impact how we're able to listen to and carry out God's will without delay or even consideration. Partly, this is because we must discern the spirits in our hearts to ensure we are truly hearing the voice of God clearly. Additionally, having heard His voice, the disordered desires of our hearts—such as fear and selfishness—can delay or prevent us from carrying out His will. Our Lady can assist us both through her examples, which shows us what perfect docility looks like, and directly through her prayers and help, which she offers as we grow and heal in the parts of our hearts that prevent us from immediately carrying out the will of the Father.

This effective maternity of Our Lady is a sign of the maternity of the Church. This means that her motherhood and the Church's motherhood don't just act as signs, but also offer real and living motherhood to all the baptized. In the early Church, the consecrated virgins followed Mary and echoed her spiritual motherhood and fruitfulness with their own receptivity to the Holy Spirit and generativity in souls.

The Church, Marian and Petrine

Consecrated virgins today participate in the integral witness of the Church to the world, which is always "Marian and Petrine in order to correspond to her original vocation."[173] As an image of the reality of God, which is both maternal and paternal, the Church contains mothers and fathers of the Spirit in the order of celibacy for the sake of the kingdom, whose masculinity and femininity reveal the nature of God, and, together, they are fruitful in the birth of new Christians.

In other words, the Church needs mothers and fathers of souls. In the case of women, this choice to receive and live the gift of consecrated virginity means that, in the uniting of one's will with the will of God, the woman's virginity becomes totally available to God for the good of the Church. Thus, "It is deduced from this that consecrated virginity is a state in the Church, a Marian state, not less necessary for the fecundity of the Church than the ministerial state of the Priesthood in the succession of the Apostles."[174] It is right to emphasize the need for priestly vocations, but this emphasis needs to occur with a concurrent emphasis on female consecrated vocations in order for the Church to fulfill her mission, as the Petrine-Marian duality is intrinsically fruitful:

> In Peter and the other Apostles there emerges above all the aspect of fruitfulness, as it is expressed in ecclesial ministry, which becomes an instrument of the Spirit for bringing new sons and daughters to birth through the preaching of the word, the celebration of the Sacraments and the giving of pastoral care. In Mary the aspect of spousal receptivity is particularly clear; it is under this aspect that the Church, through her perfect virginal life, brings divine life to fruition within herself.... Following in the footsteps of Mary,

[173] Ratzinger, "Gift in the Church."
[174] Ibid.

> the New Eve, consecrated persons express their spiritual fruitfulness by becoming receptive to the Word, in order to contribute to the growth of a new humanity by their unconditional dedication and their living witness. Thus the Church fully reveals her motherhood both in the communication of divine grace entrusted to Peter and in the responsible acceptance of God's gift, exemplified by Mary.[175]

Mary, Teacher of Virginity

For consecrated virgins, Mary is, says St. Ambrose, the teacher of virginity.[176] John Paul II encouraged consecrated virgins to, "love Mary of Nazareth, the first fruits of Christian virginity.... In body and spirit she was fully what you long to be with all your strength: virgins in heart and body, spouses by your total and exclusive commitment to the love of Christ, mothers by the gift of the Spirit."[177] *Vita consecrata* echoes this:

> Mary in fact is the *sublime example of perfect consecration,* since she belongs completely to God and is totally devoted to him. Chosen by the Lord, who wished to accomplish in her the mystery of the Incarnation, she reminds consecrated persons of *the primacy of God's initiative.* At the same time, having given her assent to the divine Word, made flesh in her, Mary is the *model of the acceptance of grace* by human creatures. Having lived with Jesus and Joseph in the hidden years of Nazareth, and present at her Son's side at crucial

[175] *Vita consecrata,* no. 34.

[176] Ambrose, *Concerning Virgins,* chap. 2, New Advent, accessed August 7, 2024, https://www.newadvent.org/fathers/34072.htm.

[177] John Paul II, "May Christ Be Your Total Love," no. 7.

moments of his public life, the Blessed Virgin teaches unconditional discipleship and diligent service.[178]

Mary is also a powerful help in her example of perfect chastity. The saints, innumerable popes, and wise spiritual writers over the whole history of the Church have counseled those called to celibacy for the kingdom to cultivate a deep devotion to the Blessed Virgin.[179] Not only is her example of purity a witness to the possibility of perfect chastity, with God's grace, but she is also the one who is spoken of in the Protoevangelium (Gen. 3:15) as the one who will crush the head of Satan.

Many exorcists have commented on the ferocity with which the demons despise Mary, because there was no place in her where they are able to get a foothold. Every virtue in her is perfect. Every desire in her is ordered completely and perfectly toward God. It is her power, because God refuses her nothing since her only desire is to see His will accomplished and His name glorified, that the demons hate. She is a human being who gives birth to all that is good and holy, and her care for her children and her powerful intercession has more power than they will ever have.

Devotion to Mary is, I would suggest, an indispensable means of protection for virginal chastity, because the demons also hate those who look like Mary and who reveal to the world the goods that are revealed in Mary.[180] The most beautiful thing is that Mary desires to give us her protection and to wrap her mantle of protection around us. She can show us the areas of our hearts that are weak and vulnerable to attack, and her tenderness toward us is without limit.

[178] *Vita consecrata*, no. 28.
[179] *Sacra virginitas*, no. 64.
[180] Ibid.

Practical Applications: Growing in Relationship with Mary

We have seen in the quotes above that Mary shows us what it means to love Christ exclusively, to be a disciple and a spiritual mother, to be a completely willing servant of God, to cultivate and protect our chastity, and to be radically open to His grace. However, having Mary as the teacher of virginity is not just about seeing her example and, with God's grace, imitating her. In the same way as discipleship requires us not simply to know *about* Christ, but to *know* Christ, we are called to *know* Mary and to cultivate a real relationship with her.

Since my own consecration, I've experienced a growing closeness with Mary. Much of this has come with meditating on the Scriptures where she speaks a word I need to hear, and, not surprisingly, these words are always ones that help me to love the Lord more and to receive His love more freely. A personal example of this happened for me during an annual silent retreat. There was a beautiful moment that I was meditating on the Passion and, as I was praying, I found myself standing on top of Golgotha and watching as Jesus came over the hill, carrying His Cross. I felt a resistance in myself that was almost a disbelief that He could be doing this all for me—like my heart wouldn't receive the gift. I saw that Mary was standing next to me and I just said, "I need you to help me receive this." I was expecting her to start talking about how Jesus' love is trustworthy, or other convincing kinds of arguments to persuade me of His love, but instead, she said, "You know, He talks about you all the time. He loves the way you laugh and your sense of humor, and He loves having you near Him. He thinks your heart is beautiful." She continued sharing those things, and it was like her words cut through every barrier I was experiencing and gave me a new freedom to receive Jesus' love there on Calvary.

Mary is like this for all of us—one who knows exactly how to speak to our heart to help us love her Son and to receive His love more deeply. We all need to experience a kind of conversion to Mary's motherly heart. Just as we grow in our relationship with Our Lord, so we grow in our relationship with Our Mother. We speak so often of spending time with Jesus in prayer, and this is essential, but we can also spend time with Mary in prayer and let her be Our Mother. Mother Teresa has been quoted as recommending that we call on Mary frequently and say, "Mary, mother of Jesus, please be a mother to me now."[181] Who better than Mary, who knows the depths of the heart of her Son, can help us know and love Him more?

Let us turn together to the prayer given at the close of *Ecclesiae Sponsae Imago:*

> We praise you,
> Virgin Mother of God
> Woman of the covenant,
> of expectation and fulfilment.
> Be the mother and teacher
> of consecrated virgins,
> so that imitating you
> they will receive the Gospel joyfully
> and every day
> with humility and wonder
> discover in it
> the holy origin
> of their spousal vocation.

[181] Cerith Gardiner, "Try Mother Teresa's 5-Second Prayer When Needing Support," Aleteia, last updated July 20, 2023, https://aleteia.org/2020/12/13/try-mother-teresas-5-second-prayer-to-mary-for-when-you-need-support.

Virgin of virgins,
sealed fountain,
gate of heaven,
inspire and accompany
these sisters of ours,
may they have the gift
of spiritual discernment
pilgrims in history
may they live the dynamism
of prophecy
with freedom and courage
with determination and tenderness.

Woman full of grace,
overflowing with charity,
Virgin become Church
bless their journey
so that hope
enlightens their minds
and opens their hearts
guiding every step
and faith
makes their hands industrious
and creative
so may their lives be fruitful
and anticipating here and now
the reality of the Kingdom,
may they generate
and build up the people of God
sharing in its mission
kingly, prophetic and priestly.

We proclaim you blessed
woman of the Magnificat
mother of the living Gospel.
We pray for these sisters.
Gather them in your song
involve them in your dance
so that they follow the Lamb
wherever he goes
with lamps alight.
May they lead us also
to the eternal wedding banquet,
to the final embrace
with the Love
that never ends.[182]

[182] *Ecclesiae Sponsae Imago*, no. 115.

Questions and Scriptures for Reflection

1. How has Mary been present in my life and vocation?

2. What does Mary teach me about virginity? How can I strengthen my devotion to her and know her better?

3. Spend some time with Our Lady immediately following the birth of Jesus when all is still.

4. Pray with the appearance of Jesus, first to His Mother Mary, on the morning of the resurrection.

Isaiah 7:10–13
Luke 1:26–38
Luke 1:39–56
Luke 2:15–19
Luke 2:22–35
John 2:2–12

8

Spiritual Motherhood

The virginity of Mary became Christian virginity at the same moment in which it became motherhood.[183]

Your total and exclusive love for Christ does not deter you from loving all men and women, your brothers and sisters, because the horizons of your charity precisely because you belong to the Lord—are Christ's own horizons. According to the Apostle, the virgin "is anxious about the affairs of the Lord, how to be holy in body and spirit" (1 Cor 7:34); *she seeks the "things that are above, where Christ is seated at God's right hand"* (Col 3: 1). *But that does not make you strangers to the great values of creation and to the sufferings of humanity, nor to the suffering of the earthly city, to its conflicts and sorrows caused by war, hunger, disease, from the widespread "culture of death". Have a merciful heart and share in the sufferings of your brethren. Commit yourselves to the defense of life, to the advancement of women and to respect for their freedom and dignity. You know it: "You who are virgins for Christ" become "mothers in the spirit"* (Ordo consecrationis virginum, *n. 16), by lovingly co-operating in the evangelization of Man and in his advancement.*[184]

183 Ratzinger, "Gift in the Church."
184 John Paul II, "May Christ Be Your Total Love," no. 6.

The Crisis of Motherhood

During a trip to New York, I was very blessed to spend some time with Mother Agnes Mary Donovan, the foundress of the Sisters of Life. I shared with her how grateful I am for her yes to the Lord, which resulted in my benefiting from the spiritual motherhood of many of the sisters, and which was truly instrumental in allowing me to receive the gift of my own vocation. We talked for awhile and then, as I was leaving, as if this charism of life can't help but escape from her, she said, "Have a safe drive! And remember that you are a gift!" Her spiritual motherhood, and that of the order she founded, has profoundly changed countless lives, including mine.

On that same trip, I was able to go to the first vows of a former student I worked with during my time in campus ministry. I had been blessed to walk with her as she sensed a call to consecrated life and went through the process of joining the Salesians. Following the first profession Mass, we were able to spend some time together and she shared about her experience of entering religious life and the things that God has done in her over these past few years. She also thanked me for my own spiritual motherhood and the gift it was to her during her discernment. It was a profound gift from the Lord to see how spiritual motherhood has been transformative in my life, both in receiving its fruits and in offering it to others.

In many ways, there is a crisis of motherhood and fatherhood in our time. *Vita consecrata* says, "There is a need for people able to show the fatherly face of God and the motherly face of the Church, people who spend their lives so that others can have life and hope."[185] However, because of both the failures of physical mothers and fathers as well as the failures of those in the Church who *should* have been spiritual mothers and fathers, there

[185] *Vita consecrata*, no. 105.

are many who carry significant trauma related to motherhood and fatherhood. We can think of those who suffered abuse at the hands of clergy, but this also encompasses all those whose faith was severely negatively impacted by the abuse scandal. Even for those whose parents were wonderful mothers and fathers, no parent is perfect and we all carry to a greater or lesser extent wounds associated with the failure of our parents to love us as God loves us.

In the hiddenness of consecrated virginity, there is a powerful potential for mothering those whose hearts are closed to maternity by wounds received at the hands of their own mothers or others whose spiritual motherhood did not accurately convey the meanings proper to it. For someone who suffered abuse of any form at the hands of their mother or a mother-figure, or for those who have a tainted view of the motherhood of the Church because of the failings of her members, a religious sister may represent harm for that person instead of safety. Within the secular world, a religious sister can also be readily associated with the moral teachings of the Church, and those who are hostile to such teachings may immediately close their hearts to the gift of the sister's spiritual maternity.

This defensiveness toward those who are visibly identifiable as spiritual mothers is not universal—there may be some whose healing regarding wounds of being mothered in harmful ways comes *precisely from* those who are visibly living spiritual motherhood. However, for some, receiving the gifts of spiritual motherhood may be more possible when they are coming from one who is not immediately recognized *as* a spiritual mother. For this reason, both those who exercise their spiritual maternity through visible channels and those who exercise it in a hidden manner are necessary to respond to the crisis of motherhood that exists in the world today. Consecrated virgins play their part in this healing by offering a concealed spiritual motherhood that is capable of subverting barriers that may be impermeable to those in other forms of consecrated life.

Motherhood Is the Vocation of Every Woman

At the Cross, Jesus gave Mary to His beloved disciple as his mother and gave His beloved disciple to Mary as her son (John 19:25–27). We understand this to be the moment that Christ made His mother the Mother of all who would be born of His Church. All who are reborn to life through Baptism call her Mother, and it's from her maternal intercession that we both come to maturity and learn how to be mothers to others in turn.

To be sure, every woman has the vocation to be a mother; all express a spiritual maternity, and some also participate in physical maternity. Those who exercise their motherhood "in the Spirit" are not just those in consecrated life; it also includes those who will not have physical children, such as women who remain single or married women who experience infertility. Further, women who do become physical mothers also express a spiritual motherhood external to their family to others who are in need of seeing the tender face of God. Though it is right to call God our Father, we also recognize that God cannot be anthropomorphized and brought down into the binary reality of human beings. Scripture clearly speaks about the motherly aspects of God's love, and it is in these realities that women participate.

We can also obviously learn a great deal from physical motherhood—the two forms of maternity inform each other in profound ways. I remember when I visited my sister shortly after my first nephew was born. It was like she had gone overnight from the sister I always knew to someone who was willingly choosing to lay down every comfort in a radical way for the sake of this little being. The first night of my visit, I woke up in the middle of the night to hear my sister saying to my newborn nephew, "I don't know what you want, my love," and going into her room, I saw her trying to feed the fussy little baby. Once he was eating, we were talking quietly, and she fell asleep in the middle of a sentence. And she was the one who had been talking! She was truly pouring herself out until she had no more to pour.

We learn from physical motherhood about sacrifice, patience, balance, tenderness, fortitude, wisdom, and so much more. This also works in the opposite direction: physical motherhood learns from spiritual motherhood—particularly that spiritual motherhood expressed by consecrated women—the primacy of devotion to God that supplies for the mission He gives, generous self-gift, and so much more. In both physical and spiritual motherhood, though in different ways, woman are invited into the mystery of the redemption of Christ to say along with Him, "This is my body given for you" (Luke 22:19).

In virginity for the sake of the kingdom, spiritual motherhood is also described as motherhood according to the Spirit.

> Virginity according to the Gospel *means renouncing marriage and thus physical motherhood.* Nevertheless, the renunciation of this kind of motherhood, a renunciation that can involve great sacrifice for a woman, makes possible a different kind of motherhood: motherhood "according to the Spirit" (cf. Rom 8:4). For virginity does not deprive a woman of her prerogatives. Spiritual motherhood takes on many different forms.... *In this way a consecrated woman finds her Spouse,* different and the same in each and every person, according to his very words: "As you did it to one of the least of these my brethren, you did it to me" (Mt 25:40). Spousal love

> always involves a special readiness to be poured out for the sake of those who come within one's range of activity. In marriage this readiness, even though open to all, consists mainly in the love that parents give to their children. In virginity this readiness is open *to all people, who are embraced by the love of Christ the Spouse.*[186]

A special characteristic of the spiritual motherhood of consecrated virgins is related to the wideness of the vocation. Consecrated virgins express their spiritual motherhood in the geographical and communal spheres where God has placed us in such a way that our hearts are constantly vigilant and open to allowing the Lord to express His love to whomever He chooses through our spiritual motherhood. The expression of spiritual motherhood is also tied into the particular gifts, professions and activities of each woman such that the motherhood of the Church is extended into corners of the secular world that may not be reached by those in any other vocation.

The Fruitfulness of Spiritual Motherhood

Motherhood cannot be discussed without references to its natural consequence, which is fruit. In the realm of physical motherhood, this is revealed in the generative capacity of the spousal union for begetting children. In the realm of the spirit, it is Mary's motherhood that is illustrative with respect to fruit. In her very person, Mary links virginity and motherhood.[187] Motherhood, either in the physical sense or otherwise, is tied to fruitfulness, and virgin-

[186] *Mulieris dignitatem*, no. 21.

[187] "Virginal, Feminine, Spousal Love for Christ," 97.

ity and fecundity can be understood as inseparable because they were united in the Blessed Virgin. Fr. Raniero Cantalamessa says,

> It is apparent from everything we have said that virginity does not mean sterility. On the contrary, it signifies the utmost fruitfulness, obviously on a different, higher level than the physical. The first time virginity appears in salvation history, it is associated with the birth of a child: "A virgin shall conceive and bear a Son" (Is 7:14). Tradition has noted this link and constantly associates the title of virgin with that of mother.[188]

This is also reflected in the marriage of Mary and Joseph, where "only Mary and Joseph, who lived the mystery of His birth, became the first witnesses of a fruitfulness different from that of the flesh, that is, the fruitfulness of the Spirit."[189]

The fruitfulness of spiritual motherhood is present in the consecrated virgin by virtue of her spousal relationship with Christ:

> The spousal union thus reveals its generative capacity, manifesting the abundance of divine grace. In imitation of the Church, whose daughters they are, consecrated virgins open themselves to the gift of spiritual maternity, becoming co-operators with the Spirit. Spiritual maternity is the gift of fruitful and hospitable interiority, that in relationships with others is a caring and courageous guardian of human dignity. It is an educative wisdom that seeks to offer favourable conditions for an encounter with God, and introduces and accompanies the journey along the paths of the Spirit.[190]

[188] Cantalamessa, *Virginity: A Positive Approach*, 15.

[189] John Paul II, *Man and Woman He Created Them*, no. 75.2.

[190] *Ecclesiae Sponsae Imago*, no. 25.

The homily from the Rite of Consecration echoes this, "You have renounced marriage for the sake of Christ. Your motherhood will be motherhood of the spirit, as you do the will of your Father and work with others in a spirit of charity, so that a great family of children may be born, or reborn, to the life of grace."[191]

How can we embrace this spiritual motherhood and its fruitfulness as consecrated virgins? The answer is simple: we share in the fecundity of the Church and the Blessed Virgin by doing the will of the Father. Fruitfulness in the spiritual order is the same for all persons in that love is inherently generative and life-giving, but for consecrated virgins, as for the Church and Our Lady, fruitfulness is directed toward the birth of souls:

> There is, therefore, no reason why the virgins of God be sad, because themselves also cannot, keeping their virginity, be mothers of the flesh. For Him alone could virginity give birth to with fitting propriety, Who in His Birth could have no peer. However, that Birth of the Holy Virgin is the ornament of all holy virgins; and themselves together with Mary are mothers of Christ, if they do the will of His Father.[192]

Christ indicates this when He says, "For whoever does the will of my Father in heaven is my brother and sister and mother" (Matt. 12:50).

St. Gregory of Nyssa says something similar, in that the spiritual maternity of the virgin means that she conceives immortal children through the work of the Holy Spirit.[193] To do the will of

[191] "Homily," in *Rite of Consecration of a Virgin Living in the World*, no. 16.

[192] Augustine, *On Virginity*, pt. 5.

[193] Gregory of Nyssa, *On Virginity*, chap. 13.

the Father means relying on Christ, who always knows the will of the Father and shares it with us, one spouse to another. The final blessing at the end of the Rite of Consecration to a Life of Virginity Lived in the World says, "May the Lord Jesus, who unites to himself the hearts of sacred virgins in a nuptial covenant, make your hearts fruitful by the word that is God's seed."[194] It's the union of the heart of Christ with the heart of the consecrated virgin that makes possible the overflowing of love to others. It is a nuptial covenant, where the woman and Jesus exist, one given completely to the other, in a way that provides an unshakeable foundation for generativity.

This union of hearts always exists in freedom. Once we become aware of the will of the Father, there is a need to respond with our own *fiat* after the example of Mary's, through which the Word was made flesh. However, it is not a single yes to Christ that results in our ability to be spiritual mothers, and for this we also look to Mary as a model. Through Mary's *fiat*, Christ was conceived, and through her ongoing *fiat* He was nurtured in her womb, was born, was raised with great tenderness and protected by her obedience to the will of the Father, was accompanied faithfully in His Passion and death, and was met with deep joy at His resurrection. Her faithful *fiats* formed the foundation for Christ's life and made His saving work possible. Even now, her continued yes to the will of the Father gives birth to souls through her maternal care and intercession. We are called to imitate her example and. with our yes, to walk with others to the font of Baptism and beyond.

[194] "Solemn Blessing," in *Rite of Consecration of a Virgin Living in the World*, chap. 1, no. 36.

Self-Knowledge and the Freedom to Love

There are many practical pastoral considerations to living the vocation of consecrated virginity well, and many of them are directly (or at least tangentially) related to spiritual motherhood because they involve receiving people well and giving birth to life in them. Self-knowledge is key in responsibly living as a consecrated virgin. For example, if you have a propensity to monopolize conversations, or a tendency to problem solve in response to every person's sharing from the heart with you, or a lack of knowledge about the things that make you cranky, then spiritual maternity will be affected to some degree. To know ourselves well is to choose how we *respond* to things happening in and around us instead of *reacting*; these are very different. A response is considered while a reaction is instinctive, and while we cannot always have the space to choose a response in every situation, the more we come to know how and why we think and act the way we do, the more we can account for our shortcomings in the way we love others.

Coming to know ourselves involves, unsurprisingly, going within our hearts to the interior of our person and allowing the Lord to reveal us to ourselves. This can be difficult since it's where we discover our insufficiencies, brokenness, and sinfulness. The beautiful thing about God and healing, though, is that when He brings something up, He intends to do something about it! If He were to reveal all our weaknesses at the same time, it would leave us overwhelmed and paralyzed with despair. However, God reveals our own hearts to us gently, and with great care and timing. He also reveals us to ourselves in the measure that we know we are loved; we cannot look at the dark corners of our own soul unless we know that we will not be abandoned there, and that what lurks there is already known to the One who desires our freedom.

This process of self-knowledge and growth are lifelong; we will continue undergoing this process of healing until such time as God calls us home to Himself (and even then, we may undergo the purifying healing of purgatory). Since this is the case, we need to come to terms with the fact that we will, at times, act in a way that is contrary to our spiritual motherhood. We will love imperfectly. However, the Lord is gracious in using even our imperfect efforts because of His great love for those we are *trying* to love, and He desires the exercise of our spiritual maternity to be sanctifying both for us and for them. Part of growing in our own self-understanding is realizing that God can (and does) make up for our weaknesses. In fact, the Lord makes up for our faults quite often! Perfection is not necessary in order to be a good spiritual mother. If this were the case, Our Lady would be the only living being who could fulfill such a role.

Practical Applications: Accounting for Our Weaknesses

Even though the vocation of consecrated virginity is hidden with respect to the lack of habit or other identifying garb, it has surprised me how quickly people open up and share things with me, even having just met them. It is notably different from before my consecration, and is, I think, a very clear manifestation of the reality of spiritual motherhood. For example, at one parish social gathering, I spoke with a woman (who had no idea that I was a consecrated virgin) and within two to three minutes of speaking, she was sharing her heartbreak as a result of divorce and her hopes for restoring her marriage. It was clear that the Holy Spirit was there and guiding the conversation, and I felt the Lord guiding me in the way I was able to receive her and in the encouragement I was able to give. I'm not alone in this kind of encounter—many other consecrated virgins I've spoken with have also experienced them!

A helpful tip, especially for sensitive conversations that delve deeply into people's hearts, is to consider pastoral response in terms of three levels.[195] The first level refers to a response that only seems pastoral but is not actually helpful. For example, if a woman lost a child during pregnancy, a level one response would be, "At least you know you can have children!" Such a response is insensitive and doesn't appreciate the pain that the woman is feeling for her lost child. A level two response is something that acknowledges what another is feeling and recognizes someone else's experience and pain. In the same situation of losing a child, a level two response would be, "I'm so sorry for your loss, I know you were so excited to have this child." A level three response is one that offers the same compassion as a level two but includes some deeper indication that you were listening well to what was being shared, whether it was something audibly said or reasonably inferred. In the scenario regarding pregnancy loss it could be something like, "It really sounds like you have such a beautiful desire for motherhood; I know you've been trying so hard to have a child—I'm so sorry for your loss." Level one responses should be avoided, level two responses are adequate, but level three responses are the ones for which we should aim.

However, we know that we love imperfectly. This means that, at various points, our responses to and interactions with people who are—whether known to them or not—seeking to receive our spiritual maternity will be lacking in some way. Recognizing this, an excellent practice is to pray before an interaction or conversation

[195] Josephine Lombardi, Pastoral Counselling Lecture 12, St. Augustine Seminary, December 5, 2019.

with someone, even if it's a quick, "Come, Holy Spirit!" as someone walks our way. It fosters a healthy dependence on the Lord and reminds us that we can rely on His grace to love well. In line with this, after a conversation, another important practice is to ask the Lord to root in the person's heart anything that was good, true, and beautiful and to let anything else fall away (including anything that may have potentially been inadvertently harmful to the person during the conversation).

The reason I suggest the terms good, true, and beautiful is that they are known as the transcendentals, the eternal attributes of God that He possesses in their fullness, and which all created things reflect in some way. They are modes of being attracted to God and the things of God, and each person is generally and particularly drawn to God through one of these. For example, I am drawn to God through beauty. When I see a beautiful seascape or hear beautiful music or step inside a beautiful cathedral, my heart is lifted up and turned to God who is the source of the beauty that I'm encountering. With respect to a post-conversation prayer, a request for whatever was good, true, and beautiful to take root in the person's heart is essentially asking for the Lord to make use of whatever will draw that person to Him most powerfully.

On the fiftieth anniversary of the promulgation of the revised Rite of Consecration of Virgins, Pope Francis exhorted consecrated virgins to, "Be women of mercy, experts in humanity."[196] As we grow in this expertise, we can use various scaffolds as a framework,

[196] Francis, "Message of His Holiness Pope Francis on the Fiftieth Anniversary of the Promulgation of the Revised Rite of Consecration of Virgins" (May 31, 2020), no. 3, https://www.vatican.va/content/francesco/en/messages/pont-messages/2020/documents/papa-francesco_20200531_messaggio-50-rito consacrazione-vergini.html.

such as reading or formation tools that help us to understand the human condition, our hearts, and where the two meet in a deeper way; but we need to reconcile ourselves with the fact that we are always a work in progress with respect to our capacity to love as Christ loves. The beautiful thing is that He doesn't choose us to be His brides, and spiritual mothers, because of our perfection. He has already told us that all things can be done through Him (Phil. 4:13), all things are made new in Him (2 Cor. 5:17), and that He works for the good in all things for those who love Him and are called according to His purpose (Rom. 8:28). He can use us, and does use us, as we are.

Questions and Scriptures for Reflection

1. How have I experienced the spiritual motherhood of another? How is my own spiritual maternity unique?

2. How have I experienced the motherhood of Mary?

3. Meditate on Mary's motherhood during Jesus' young life, Jesus' public ministry and Jesus' Passion.

4. What wounds do I have from my experiences with my mother or others in maternal roles?

5. How well do I know myself? Am I afraid to explore my own dark corners?

6. How can I grow to become an expert in humanity?

Luke 1:39–45
Luke 2:24–52
John 19:25–27
Romans 8:26–30
2 Corinthians 5:16–21
Philippians 4:12–13

9

The Marriage Bed of the Cross

In the different forms of life inspired by the Spirit throughout history, consecrated persons discover that the more they stand at the foot of the Cross of Christ, the more immediately and profoundly they experience the truth of God who is love. It is precisely on the Cross that the One who in death appears to human eyes as disfigured and without beauty, so much so that the bystanders cover their faces (cf. Is 53:2–3), fully reveals the beauty and power of God's love. Saint Augustine says: "Beautiful is God, the Word with God.... He is beautiful in heaven, beautiful on earth; beautiful in the womb, beautiful in his parents' arms, beautiful in his miracles, beautiful in his sufferings; beautiful in inviting to life, beautiful in not worrying about death, beautiful in giving up his life and beautiful in taking it up again; he is beautiful on the Cross, beautiful in the tomb, beautiful in heaven. Listen to the song with understanding, and let not the weakness of the flesh distract your eyes from the splendour of his beauty." The consecrated life reflects the splendour of this love because, by its fidelity to the mystery of the Cross, it confesses that it believes and lives by the love of the Father, Son and Holy Spirit. In this way it helps the Church to remain aware that the Cross is the superabundance of God's love poured out upon this world, and that it is the great sign of Christ's saving presence, especially in the midst of difficulties and trials.[197]

[197] *Vita consecrata*, no. 24.

Foundations for Understanding Suffering

It might seem odd to include a chapter on suffering in a book that is centered around the theology of consecrated virginity. However, an image comes to mind that poignantly expresses the centrality of suffering for those in consecrated life. During a "Come and See" visit that I once had with the Religious Sisters of Mercy of Alma, I noticed that their community cross didn't have a corpus on it. Rather, it was just an inner white cross with a black outline around it. When I asked why this was, the Sister answered that their cross symbolized the meeting of the misery of humanity (the black outline) with the mercy of God (the inner white cross), and that the Sister herself becomes the corpus of the cross where the misery of Man and the mercy of God meet. It was a powerful witness of the reality of consecrated life, which always entails deep intimacy with a Divine, crucified Spouse. Especially for the consecrated virgin, who is mystically betrothed to the One who inseparably links the Cross to the resurrection, a faulty understanding of suffering *is* an errant understanding of the heart of her Spouse. In order to live well our spousal relationship with Christ, we need to overcome fearing the Cross.

The second reading from the feast day of St. John of the Cross is my favorite from among the Office of Readings in the Liturgy of the Hours. He speaks eloquently of the mystery of redemptive suffering and the treasures that we find when we "dig deeply in Christ":

> Would that men might come at last to see that it is quite impossible to reach the thicket of the riches and wisdom of

> God except by first entering the thicket of much suffering, in such a way that the soul finds there its consolation and desire. The soul that longs for divine wisdom chooses first, and in truth, to enter the thicket of the cross.
>
> Saint Paul therefore urges the Ephesians not to grow weary in the midst of tribulations, but to be steadfast and rooted and grounded in love, so that they may know with all the saints the breadth, the length, the height and the depth—to know what is beyond knowledge, the love of Christ, so as to be filled with all the fullness of God.
>
> The gate that gives entry into these riches of his wisdom is the cross; because it is a narrow gate, while many seek the joys that can be gained through it, it is given to few to desire to pass through it.[198]

The Cross permeates the entirety of human life with its hope, because human life is infused with suffering. God knew the remedy to sin that would come in the form of a cross, and even into the human body He has built the shape of the Cross.[199] However, any time we speak of suffering, we need to affirm its inherent mystery. Philosophers and theologians across the ages have sought to make sense of suffering, and there are indeed many things we can know about suffering, especially in light of Christ's own suffering, death and resurrection. At the same time, suffering remains a stumbling block and one of the deepest questions that surfaces in the heart of the human person. Why does suffering exist? If God is good, why does He allow suffering, and especially the suffering of the

[198] John of the Cross, *From a Spiritual Canticle of St John of the Cross, priest*, Liturgies.net, accessed March 25, 2021, https://www.liturgies.net/saints/johnofthecross/readings.htm.

[199] Justin Martyr, *First Apology*, no. 55.

innocent? We'll shed some light on these questions in this chapter, but we also need to read with a heart open to the mystery of God. In a similar way to the Holy Trinity, God has revealed many things about suffering, but as St. John of the Cross indicates, there is no limit of depth when we're considering God and His mysteries.

I highly recommend taking the time to read *Salvifici doloris*, the apostolic letter of John Paul II on the Christian meaning of human suffering, which I've used as the main source for this chapter. John Paul II shares beautifully about the meaning of suffering, even to the point of being able to say that, suffering "is something good, before which the Church bows down in reverence with all the depth of her faith in the Redemption."[200] This is a hard sentence to swallow, but part of the possibility of accepting it is to look to the one who wrote it. John Paul II was not a man unacquainted with suffering. He lost both of his parents when he was young, lived through World War II in Poland under the Nazi regime where he endured hard labor in devastating conditions and saw the horrors of oppression firsthand, experienced persecution from many corners, then became Pope and was shot, yet survived, and in the end suffered and died from Parkinson's disease. His life was surely such that he could have become lost in despair, but on the contrary, his closeness to the cross of Christ allowed him to see, up close, the beauty of the Saviour's love and its inseparability with the hope of the resurrection.

To understand suffering, and even more, redemptive suffering, we need to build some clear definitions. All suffering is a contact with evil. In fact, in the Old Testament there is no word that directly translates as suffering, but rather the word used to

[200] John Paul II, *Salvifici Doloris: Apostolic Letter on the Christian Meaning of Human Suffering* (Pauline Books and Media, 2005), no. 24.

describe instances of suffering is the word evil.[201] Since suffering is a contact with evil, our tendency to recoil from it makes a great deal of sense. John Paul II puts it even more dramatically: "Suffering is the undergoing of evil before which Man shudders."[202] However, suffering and evil are not *things* in themselves, but are rather the experiences of a lack, limitation or distortion of a good that we don't share in.[203] When we are sick, we are suffering from a lack of health. When we grieve over someone, we are making contact with the evil of death and experiencing the lack of the person's presence. When we are hungry, we are suffering from a lack of food.

We also experience suffering in the double-dimension of the human person, who is a soul-body composite. Bodily suffering is related to the physical, corporeal reality of Man, and the suffering of the soul is called moral suffering; though we can delineate between these two sources of suffering, the experience of suffering encapsulates the whole person because Man cannot divide his soul from his body or his body from his soul.[204] It's also important to note that, in most cases, moral suffering is much harder to remedy because it is much more hidden and abstract than physical suffering.

When thinking about suffering, it's also crucial to delineate *how* we come to suffer with respect to the will of God. Most importantly, *God does not directly will our suffering.* Theology tells us that He has two forms of will: His perfect will and His permissive will. Without getting too bogged down in the distinction between

[201] Ibid., no. 7.
[202] Ibid., no. 18.
[203] Ibid., no. 7.
[204] Ibid., no. 5.

the two, a simplified way to distinguish them is to think of God's perfect will as His direct willing of things, such as our coming into and remaining in existence, and His permissive will as what He allows in order not to violate Man's free will. It is necessary for us to retain our free will at all times, because it is what allows us to love; we cannot make the choice to love unless there is freedom to choose not to love, otherwise, love would be devoid of its substantial meaning. Most human suffering can be traced to Man's propensity to abuse his free will: suffering person to person and self-inflicted suffering account for much of the suffering in the world. However, even in the case of the suffering caused by natural disasters (though some of Man's influence can be traced directly to these) or in things like developing cancer despite refraining from activities that contribute to it, there is still a link to free will. It was free will that allowed sin's existence in the first place, and this Original Sin introduced disorder into the very fabric of creation. Now, we live in a fallen world that is intrinsically disordered, and even the disorder of creation can bring Man suffering under many different facets.

In light of these two expressions of the will of God, we can say that God does not will our suffering according to His perfect will, because He is only love and love always wills the good of the beloved. We *can* say that God allows our suffering according to His permissive will, and that, *precisely because* He is good, He can use the suffering that we experience for our good. This is affirmed by St. Paul: "And we know that in all things God works for the good of those who love him, who have been called according to his purpose" (Rom. 8:28). St. Alphonsus Liguori expresses it in light of gift and says that the good things we experience are to be received as gifts from God for our delight, and that the bad things we experience are to be received as gifts from God that are ordered to our growth in holiness.[205] God is able to use all suffering for our good, regardless of how it comes to us (even the consequences of our own sin, where repentance is present!).

Simply because we say that suffering can be something good doesn't mean that we are meant to leave others in their sufferings or seek it out for ourselves. Suffering will come to all of us, and we are always called to relieve suffering where possible, which we can see modeled in the Parable of the Good Samaritan (Luke 10:29–37). Even with respect to our own chosen sufferings in the form of mortification, we need to be careful to take on only the things the Lord is asking us to; excessive mortifications can become counterproductive and a gateway for spiritual pride to enter. Some people who experience suffering that could be lessened feel called to endure the pain they are experiencing and not to remedy it, but this is the exception and not the rule. The Lord very carefully chooses the crosses that He desires us to carry, and it is prudent to discern with a spiritual director how we're being called to respond to our sufferings, chosen or otherwise.

There are two aspects intrinsic to our crosses: suffering in solidarity and suffering in dispersion.[206] Solidarity in suffering refers to the communion that can be experienced by those who suffer in a similar way. Grief or cancer support groups would be examples of this. Suffering in dispersion is connected to what John Paul II calls the personalistic norm. The personalistic norm, simply put, is that we are all unique human persons created by God who

205 Alphonsus Liguori, *Uniformity with God's Will* (The Catholic Primer, 2006), 8, last modified 2006, https://www.basilica.ca/documents/2016/10/St.%20Alphonsus%20Liguori-Uniformity%20with%20Gods%20Will.pdf.

206 *Salvifici doloris*, no. 8.

cannot be replaced, one for another, and who can never be used in a utilitarian way; the only proper response to the human person is love.[207] With respect to suffering, it is exactly the unique and unrepeatable nature of each person that prevents any two experiences of suffering from being completely alike, even when the suffering stems from the same source. This results in the experience of suffering in dispersion.

When I encountered deep suffering in my life a number of years ago, I remember feeling an overwhelming isolation. It felt as though, no matter how well I explained what I was experiencing or how much I desired to be accompanied in my suffering, the deepest parts of my experience were impenetrable. Upon discovering *Salvifici doloris* and John Paul II's description of suffering in dispersion, instead of feeling a despair about my pain-induced loneliness, I felt a great comfort in knowing that there wasn't something wrong with me. Rather, it was a discovery that even the pain of suffering points to the beautiful uniqueness of the human person. It was also a discovery that suffering is an intimate place of union with the Lord, who is the only one who can penetrate our suffering to its depths. Even more, it is in these precise places of solitude that the Lord invites us into His own experience of suffering.

Human suffering, and particularly the dispersive effect of human suffering, causes the person to utter this question: "Why?"[208] It is the same question uttered by Job, a man described as righteous (i.e. without sin) who is experiencing terrible suffering. Up to this point in the Scriptures, suffering has been associated with sin,

[207] Karol Wojtyla, *Love and Responsibility*, trans. Grzegorz Ignatik (Pauline Books and Media, 2013), 25.

[208] *Salvifici doloris*, no. 9.

in that it is seen as the just consequence of transgressing God's laws. Job's friends, therefore, spend a good deal of time trying to convince him to accept that he has sinned and don't believe his protestations to the contrary. Job's experience doesn't negate the punitive element to suffering, but it does point out that suffering is not always the result of personal sin. The longest recorded discourse of God with Man in the Scriptures is in the book of Job, and in it, God affirms that Job is innocent but also indicates that the vision of Man is limited, and we cannot know the reasons for all of the sufferings that we experience. In the end, Job's fortunes are restored, but we are left with a new view of the reasons we suffer, which, though we understand some aspects of suffering, are still largely hidden in mystery. It is imperative to note that God doesn't respond to Job's suffering with answers, but He *does* respond to Job's suffering with His *presence*. God answers the question of suffering with His very self and, ultimately, in the suffering of His Son.[209]

The Redemptive Meaning of Suffering

Looking to Christ, we come to the redemptive meaning of suffering. When Christ enters into the very depths of suffering, because He has gone there to accomplish the redemption of Man, He changes the definition of suffering and links it to redemption: "In the Cross of Christ not only is the Redemption accomplished through suffering, but *also human suffering itself has been redeemed*.... In bringing about the Redemption through suffering, Christ *has* also *raised human suffering to the level of Redemption*."[210]

[209] Ibid., no. 13.
[210] Ibid., no. 19.

The Paschal mystery of the suffering, death, and resurrection of Christ has always been seen as a united movement by the Church, because no element of the three makes sense without the other two. They are tied together. So much so that the liturgies of Holy Thursday, Good Friday, and Easter are seen as one single liturgical action. As a result, the meaning of the redemption that Christ accomplishes through suffering is also tied intrinsically to meanings of salvation, resurrection, and glory. These are all accomplished by God, who is love and accomplishes them in love; therefore, the very meaning of human suffering itself has been changed and forever linked to these meanings:

> Human suffering has reached its culmination in the Passion of Christ. And at the same time it has entered into a completely new dimension and a new order: *it has been linked to love,* to that love of which Christ spoke to Nicodemus, to that love which creates good, drawing it out by means of suffering, just as the supreme good of the Redemption of the world was drawn from the Cross of Christ, and from that Cross constantly takes its beginning.[211]

Therefore, "Suffering is, in itself, an experience of evil. But Christ has made suffering the firmest basis of the definitive good, namely the good of eternal salvation."[212] We can start to see here the rationale for how suffering can, somehow, be called a good.

This is not the end of the meaning of redemptive suffering. From the very beginning of Man's existence, he has been invited into the creative capacities of God as a co-creator. We can see this in God's invitation to Adam to cultivate the earth and to exercise

211 Ibid., no. 18.
212 Ibid., no. 26.

his dominion over it, and we see it most profoundly in Man's cooperation with the creation of new human life. It has continued throughout history in our call to the arts, to work and labor, to sanctify the world in prayer, and more. God invites us to be sharers in His divine life in every aspect—including in His suffering. On the Cross, Christ opened up His own sufferings to Man in an invitation to share in the redemption of the world: "Man, discovering through faith the redemptive suffering of Christ, also discovers in it his own sufferings; he *rediscovers them, through faith,* enriched with a new content and new meaning."[213]

Truly, there is joy that can be united with suffering in a mysterious way. Since Christ has linked suffering to resurrection, He has linked sorrow to joy. He has done this in His very body; He has retained the wounds of His suffering in His glorified body and constitutes in His very person the union of death and life. We participate, through our sufferings, in the joys of Christ when we offer ourselves as a gift and imitate His eucharistic offering, saying with Him, "this is my body given for you" (Luke 22:19). There is joy in participating in His redeeming mission "in order *to unleash love in the human person,*"[214] and love always has the joy of the Spirit, even when it is mysteriously cloaked in sorrow.

This is why Paul can say, "I am now rejoicing in my sufferings for your sake, and in my flesh I am completing what is lacking in Christ's afflictions for the sake of his body, that is, the church" (Col. 1:24, NRSVCE). Christ invites us to participate in the salvation of the whole world through offering our sufferings in union with His for the redemption of Man and our own sanctification.

[213] Ibid., no. 20.
[214] Ibid., no. 29.

Christ's sufferings are sufficient for Man's redemption; He closes off no part of His divine life from our participation.

Suffering and Consecrated Virginity

As spouses lay their lives down for each other and enter through inter-donation into the marital embrace, so a spouse of Christ comes to lay herself down in the very place Christ lays *His* life down, which is at the Cross. Christ's spousal love is specifically constituted by His suffering, meaning that whoever calls Him spouse enters into the marriage bed that He has established, which is the Cross.[215] The nuptial meaning of the Cross is also poignantly seen in Christ's last words, most often translated as "it is finished" (John 19:30), but more aptly translated as *consummatum est*: "it is consummated." The union of Christ with His Bride, the Church, has now been made possible precisely through self-gift in suffering, which must be true on *both ends* of the nuptial embrace: the Church as the Bride, and the consecrated virgin as bride, consummate their marriage with the Lamb on the Cross.

To be clear, all Christians are called to union with the Crucified Christ, but it is true that "virgins are obliged to own it and to live it in a more radical way, making it the substance of their daily life."[216] John Paul II affirms this when he says:

> Continence "for the kingdom of heaven"—inasmuch as it is an indubitable sign of the "other world"—bears within itself above all the inner dynamism of the mystery of the redemption of the body (see Lk 20:35), and in this meaning

[215] Cantalamessa, *Virginity: A Positive Approach*, 38.
[216] Ibid., no. 48.

> it also possesses the characteristic of a particular likeness with Christ. The one who consciously chooses such continence chooses in some sense a particular participation in the mystery of the redemption (of the body); he wishes to complete it in a particular way in his own flesh (see Col 1:24), finding thereby also the imprint of a likeness with Christ.[217]

For those called to the nuptial embrace of the Cross, it is not an embrace lacking in hope or joy. On the contrary, we've shown earlier in this chapter that the Paschal mystery has an inner cohesiveness, and therefore that it unites suffering and resurrection, sorrow and joy. Mysteriously, the union of a bride of Christ with her Crucified Spouse is also a touching of the realities of resurrection and eternal life. The living union with Christ, who carries the wounds of His death in His resurrected body, provides the means through which one espoused to Christ finds the foundation for her witness to the joy of the resurrection, even in the midst of suffering: "At the same time, because of the spousal bond with Christ, it [Christian virginity] also proclaims the beginning of the life of the world to come."[218]

To look at this point from another angle, we can go back to St. John of the Cross's description of the "thicket of much suffering." Notably, he doesn't tell us that joy comes at the cessation of crucifying experiences, but rather that the soul comes to exist in the thicket of suffering "in such a way that the soul finds there its consolation and desire." It is not a matter of making it through suffering to find joy, but of finding joy *in* suffering. It is to come

[217] John Paul II, *Man and Woman He Created Them*, no. 76.3.
[218] *Ecclesiae Sponsae Imago*, no. 17.

to see the thicket of suffering as itself beautiful. Mother Teresa has another way of putting this, "I have found the paradox, that if you love until it hurts, there can be no more hurt, only more love."[219] This is how we can say that "The message of the cross is foolishness to those who are perishing, but to us who are being saved it is the power of God" (1 Cor. 1:18).

Since suffering is present in the life of every person and often produces one of the most formidable roadblocks to belief in God, the prophetic witness of those who touch both suffering and resurrection on the marriage bed of the Cross can express the true meaning of suffering and its redemptive nature to a world that finds suffering incomprehensible. The joyful offering of one's life in consecrated celibacy prompts many questions. How is it possible for this person to have given up these normative human experiences, such as the goods of marriage and family, and still experience fulfillment? How can one who peacefully welcomes suffering in one's chosen way of life and in their personal circumstances be joyful? How is it possible to be espoused to Christ and united with Him on the Cross and still find hope in that place of darkness? This, of course, is a challenge to all who are consecrated to consider seriously what it means to suffer well, because preaching Christ Crucified without the willingness to follow after Him ourselves is dishonest. It is true that our ability to suffer well grows just as we grow in every aspect of the spiritual life, but it does require being honest with ourselves and asking the Lord for the graces to grow in our capacity to embrace His Cross.

Our witness regarding suffering is also present in the way that consecrated persons respond to others who are suffering:

[219] Teresa of Calcutta, "Mother Teresa Quotes," Catholic Online, accessed September 13, 2024, https://www.catholic.org/clife/teresa/quotes.php.

> The quest for divine beauty impels consecrated persons to care for the deformed image of God on the faces of their brothers and sisters, faces disfigured by hunger, faces disillusioned by political promises, faces humiliated by seeing their culture despised, faces frightened by constant and indiscriminate violence, the anguished faces of minors, the hurt and humiliated faces of women, the tired faces of migrants who are not given a warm welcome, the faces of the elderly who are without even the minimum conditions for a dignified life.[220]

We are called never to lose sight of the hope of the resurrection so that, even when people cannot hold onto it themselves, we can hold onto it on their behalf.

Practical Applications: Learning to Suffer Well

Ecclesiae Sponsae Image states that women who receive the consecration must exhibit "a proven aptitude to reframe suffering and frustration, and to give and receive forgiveness, as possible steps towards the fullness of human nature."[221] Since suffering and the spousal embrace of the Cross are so central to the vocation, it is necessary for us to grow in our understanding of the call to become fastened to the Cross with Christ. Learning to suffer well, spouse of Christ or not, is a matter of graduality: "*As the individual takes up his cross*, spiritually uniting himself to the Cross of Christ, the salvific meaning of suffering is revealed before him.... It is then that Man finds in his suffering interior peace and even spiritual joy."[222]

[220] *Vita consecrata*, no. 75.

[221] *Ecclesiae Sponsae Imago*, no. 87.

[222] *Salvifici doloris*, no. 26.

One of the greatest helps in learning to embrace the Cross is to grow in love for the Eucharist. The Eucharist, by virtue of its re-presentation of the Paschal mystery, is another expression of nuptial love. On the altar, Christ's sacrifice for His Bride, the Church, is re-presented, and those called to be His spouses in consecrated life consummate their nuptial union with Christ in the reception of His very body. We become one with the Bridegroom and receive from Him all the graces we need to become more and more conformed to Him. Our hearts become more like His, and we increasingly share in His love and desire for souls. Since we willingly offer our sufferings for those who are dear to us, becoming united more deeply with Christ's heart helps us to offer our sufferings for all who are dear to *Him*, which is all persons:

> The bride does not wish to know who is to benefit from the fruits of her prayers and sufferings. They belong to the Bridegroom, who gives them to whom He will. Others will have to worry about how to distribute and administer them. It is not her concern. Truly, the Lord "lets the barren woman be seated at home, the happy mother of children" (Ps. 113:9).[223]

A note on the acceptance of suffering: much of the suffering that we experience at times is self-imposed. I am tired during prayer because I stayed up too late last night; I am feeling sick because I ate too much or too little; I am lacking peace because I refuse to forgive someone who has wronged me. Whenever we encounter suffering in our lives, though we can still offer that suffering to the Lord, we should seriously consider who imposed that cross. If it is allowed by God through our circumstances and we can't do a

[223] Cantalamessa, *Virginity: A Positive Approach,* 19.

lot to remedy it (e.g. a chronic illness that we need to learn to live with), we can safely accept it with peace and offer those sufferings to the Lord in union with His. Most other sufferings—whether they are health issues we *can* do something about, or pains from a relationship, or self-imposed sufferings resulting from our own actions—require some kind of attempt at remedying. If I suffer a headache because I drank too much wine, I'm not called to continue drinking too much wine and to offer up the suffering of the headaches—I'm called to stop drinking so much wine! As with most things, spiritual directors are excellent sources for discerning areas where we may be experiencing suffering that the Lord is not asking us to continue carrying.

One very practical way to grow in our capacity to receive various unchosen crosses is the ascetical life, which is comprised, in a sense, of "chosen crosses." In fact, asceticism is foundational to consecrated life: "Asceticism, by helping to master and correct the inclinations of human nature wounded by sin, is truly indispensable if consecrated persons are to remain faithful to their own vocation and follow Jesus on the way of the Cross."[224] In religious life, each community's sacrificial practices are detailed in their constitutions (e.g. hours of additional prayer, practices for fasting, bodily mortifications, limits to use of technology), and additional sacrifices of individual members are most often undertaken with the permission of the superior and the person's spiritual director. For consecrated virgins, however, it can be a challenge to determine what ascetical practice ought to look like in the life of one who is intentionally *not* separated from the world, but who *is* called not to take on the spirit of the world.

[224] *Vita consecrata,* no. 38.

To determine what asceticism might look like, there are three immediate sources of help that can assist: other consecrated virgins, the diocesan bishop, and the spiritual director. Hearing about the experience of other consecrated virgins can be immensely helpful, particularly for those who are looking at living a more intense ascetical life for the first time. Bishops are also an excellent sounding board, as they are called to be fathers to consecrated virgins and to offer their wisdom and guidance. Spiritual directors are often the most immediate and best guides for implementing ascetic practices, because they likely know the woman most deeply and will have a sense of what practices can be adopted without running into pitfalls like spiritual pride or scrupulosity.

Finally, to understand that suffering "is something good, before which the Church bows down in reverence with all the depth of her faith in the redemption,"[225] there is no better place to be than at the side of Our Lady at the foot of the Cross. She is the one whose heart was pierced at the sight of her son's suffering, but at the same instant, never waivered in her trust in God or His goodness. The Lord desires for us to experience the freedom that we can possess when we are unafraid of our own suffering and that of others, and He has tasked Mary with helping us come to this freedom because she is right beside us while we gaze on Christ's broken body. She helps us, especially in times of profound suffering where the darkness eclipses everything but the space immediately before us, to know that every cross is tied to a resurrection in her Son.

[225] *Salvifici doloris*, no.24.

Questions and Scriptures for Reflection

1. Am I afraid of suffering? Do I run from it? How can I grow in my capacity to suffer well?

2. How would I explain redemptive suffering to someone?

3. Pray with Mary at the foot of the Cross—what does she have to say about suffering?

4. Pray with the story of Job.

John 19
1 Corinthians 1:18–25
Colossians 1:24–29

Conclusion

The themes contained in this book are by no means exhaustive, but I hope they are at least helpful in understanding more about the vocation of consecrated virginity, as well as how it fits within the ecclesial structure of the Church. Though I hope others find it useful, I have personally found it helpful to go back to the primary sources of material and pull them together to give a more complete picture of consecrated virginity. As I shared right from the beginning, it is very likely that we'll see many more resources arise in the coming years as this vocation continues to grow. In fact, it will be absolutely necessary, because where there is growth, there is an increase in "messiness" and a need for clarity!

It has been beautiful to see how many women are sensing a call to this vocation, and more generally, how much interest there is from the wider Church in understanding more about it. Canada is seeing many more women inquire about the consecration, many in dioceses where the *Ordo Virginum* is not yet established, and many of those already consecrated are coming together in the hopes of forming a national association of consecrated virgins. We have already started meeting virtually for activities such as vespers and book studies and are working toward becoming a Public Association of the Faithful. Canada is not unique in this—consecrated virginity is taking root in a beautiful way all over the world. As the vocation continues to grow, it is my hope (and that of many other consecrated virgins I've spoken with from a number of different countries) that there will be increasing collaboration between bishops and consecrated virgins for things like establishing norms for formation of aspirants and candidates and resources for ongoing formation of those already consecrated. There is great excitement in our time for the beautiful ways that consecrated virgins can be witnesses to hope in a world that desperately needs to encounter the love of Christ, the Bridegroom.

To my dear sisters in the *Ordo Virginum:* What a gift it has been to come to know many of you. In terms of my vocation, I'm still a "baby" consecrated virgin, and I have learned so much from so many of you. At a recent weekend retreat that I attended with other consecrated virgins, we noted how beautiful it was to be able to spend time together and to hear about each other's lives and the relationship that each of us has with the Lord. The same has been true for the formation gatherings that I've been part of with consecrated virginity candidates; it is such a gift to be able to spend time with other women whose lens of loving the Lord is the same as one's own, even though that love shows up differently in each person. I'm sure I speak for most of us when I say that the future of this vocation holds so much excitement! Let us pray for each other, that we will be good spouses to Our Lord and love Him with undivided hearts.

To our bishops: Thank you for your love of consecrated virginity and your desire to have the *Ordo Virginum* present in your dioceses! All things in this vocation are connected to you; without your fatherly care, the flowering of this vocation that occurred, and is now occurring with even more force, would have been extinguished. Thank you for loving Christ the Bridegroom and, with great love and concern, forming and caring for those who are called to be His brides in this vocation.

To those who are in formation or are discerning consecrated virginity: Sometimes the road to consecration is swift and full of consolation, but I think that is the exception rather than the norm! The challenge of this time is that the global Church is still determining how best to walk with those who are on their way to consecration. If it has been a long road for you, or if you are still discerning how the Lord is calling, please know that those already consecrated are praying for you, and that the Lord is faithful.

Bibliography

Ambrose of Milan. "Concerning Virgins." New Advent. Accessed August 7, 2024. https://www.newadvent.org/fathers/34072.htm.

——. "Concerning Widows." New Advent. Accessed July 10, 2024. https://www.newadvent.org/fathers/3408.htm.

Athenagoras of Athens. "A Plea for the Christians." New Advent. Accessed July 10, 2024. https://www.newadvent.org/fathers/0205.htm.

Augustine of Hippo. "Letter 211." New Advent. Accessed July 10, 2024. https://www.newadvent.org/fathers/1102211.htm.

——. "Of Holy Virginity." Accessed July 10, 2024. https://www.newadvent.org/fathers/1310.htm.

Basil of Caesarea. "Letter 199 to Amphilochius." New Advent. Accessed July 10, 2024. https://www.newadvent.org/fathers/3202199.htm.

Benedict XVI. "Address to the Participants in the International Congress-Pilgrimage of the Ordo Virginum." Delivered May

15, 2008. https://www.vatican.va/content/benedict-xvi/en/speeches/2008/may/documents/hf_ben-xvi_spe_20080515_ordo-virginum.html.

——. *Sacramentum caritatis.* Promulgated February 22, 2007. https://www.vatican.va/content/benedict-xvi/en/apost_exhortations/documents/hf_ben-xvi_exh_20070222_sacramentum-caritatis.html.

Cantalamessa, Raniero. *Virginity: A Positive Approach to Celibacy for the Sake of the Kingdom.* Translated by Charles Serignat. St. Paul's Publishing, 1995.

Catechism of the Catholic Church. Doubleday, 1994.

Code of Canon Law. Promulgated January 25, 1983. https://www.vatican.va/archive/cod-iuris-canonici/cic_index_en.html.

"The Congregation for Institutes of Consecrated Life and Societies of Apostolic Life." Vatican.va. Accessed August 2, 2024. https://www.vatican.va/roman_curia/congregations/ccscrlife/ documents/rc_con_ccscrlife_profile_en.html.

Chrysostom, John. *Commentary on Second Corinthians.* Translated by St. George Monastery, Monaxi Agapi and Anna Skoubourdis. Lulu Press, 2020.

Clement of Rome. "Epistle to the Corinthians." New Advent. Accessed July 10, 2024. https://www.newadvent.org/fathers/1010.htm.

The Cloud of Unknowing. Edited by Bernard Bangley. Paraclete Press, 2006.

Congregation for Institutes of Consecrated Life and Societies of Apostolic Life. *Ecclesiae Sponsae Imago: Instruction on the Ordo Virginum.* Libreria Editrice Vaticana, 2018.

Cooper, Jenna. "Who Can Be Called a Bride of Christ?" *Sponsa Christi.* Last updated March 1, 2015. https://sponsa-christi.blogspot.com/2015/03/who-can-be-called-bride-of-christ.html.

Cyprian of Carthage. "On the Dress of Virgins." EWTN. Accessed July 10, 2024. https://www.ewtn.com/catholicism/library/on-the-dress-of-virgins-de-habitu-virginum-11407.

De Lassus, Dom Dysmas. *Abuses in the Religious Life and the Path to Healing*. Sophia Institute Press, 2023.

Francis. "Message of His Holiness Pope Francis on the Fiftieth Anniversary of the Promulgation of the Revised Rite of Consecration of Virgins." Delivered May 31, 2020. https://www.vatican.va/content/francesco/en/messages/pont-messages/2020/documents/papa-francesco_20200531_messaggio-50-ritoconsacrazione-vergini.html.

Mother Mary Francis. *My Beloved Is Mine and I Am His: Meditations on Brideship for Women Religious*. Cluny Media, 2022.

Gardiner, Cerith. "Try Mother Teresa's 5-Second Prayer When Needing Support." Aleteia. Last modified July 20, 2023. https://aleteia.org/2020/12/13/try-mother-teresas-5-second-prayer to-mary-for-when-you-need-support.

Gregory of Nyssa. *On Virginity*. New Advent. Accessed July 10, 2024. https://www.newadvent.org/fathers/2907.htm.

Gregory the Great. "An Exposition on the Song of Songs." Lectio Divina. Accessed August 24, 2024. https://www.lectio-divina.org/images/patristics/Commentary%20on%20the%20Song%20of%20Songs%20by%20Gregory%20the%20Great.pdf.

Hahn, Scott. *A Father Who Keeps His Promises: God's Covenant Love in Scripture*. Servant, 1998.

Ignatius of Antioch. "Epistle to Polycarp." New Advent. Accessed July 10, 2024. https://www.newadvent.org/fathers/0110.htm.

———. "Epistle to the Smyrnaeans." New Advent. Accessed July 10, 2024. https://www.newadvent.org/fathers/0109.htm.

Ignatius of Loyola. "Rules for Perceiving the Movements Caused in the Soul: First Week." In *Spiritual Exercises*. Accessed July 7, 2024. https://mycatholic.life/books/the-spiritual-exercises-of-saint-ignatius-of-loyola/rules/.

John of Damascus. *An Exposition of the Orthodox Faith*. New Advent. Accessed July 10, 2024. https://www.newadvent.org/fathers/3304.htm.

John of the Cross. "From a Spiritual Canticle of St John of the Cross, Priest." Liturgies.net. Accessed March 25, 2021. https://www.liturgies.net/saints/johnofthecross/readings.htm.

John Paul II. "You Are [a] Sign of [the] Church's Virginity." Address to Consecrated Virgins. June 14, 1995. https://diolc.org/files/consecratedlife/Pope%20John%20Paul%20II%201995%20Presentation.pdf.

——. *Christifideles laici*. Promulgated December 30, 1988. https://www.vatican.va/content/john-paul-ii/en/apost_exhortations/documents/hf_jp-ii_exh_30121988_christifideles-laici.html.

——. *Man and Woman He Created Them: A Theology of the Body*. Translated by Michael Waldstein. Pauline Books & Media, 2006.

——. *Mulieris dignitatem*. Promulgated August 15, 1988. https://www.vatican.va/content/john-paul-ii/en/apost_letters/1988/documents/hf_jp-ii_apl_19880815_mulieris-dignitatem.html.

——. *Salvifici Doloris: Apostolic Letter on the Christian Meaning of Human Suffering*. Anniversary ed. Pauline Books and Media, 2005.

——. *Vita consecrata*. Promulgated March 25, 1996. https://www.vatican.va/content/john-paul-ii/en/apost_exhortations/documents/hf_jp-ii_exh_25031996_vita-consecrata.html.

Josephus. *Of the War*. Bk. 2. *Penelope*, University of Chicago. Accessed August 22, 2024. https://penelope.uchicago.edu/josephus/war-2.html.

Just, Felix, S.J. "Jewish Groups at the Time of Jesus." Last Modified October 19, 2001. https://catholic-resources.org/Bible/Jewish_Groups.htm#Essenes.

Justin Martyr. "First Apology." New Advent. Accessed July 10, 2024. https://www.newadvent.org/fathers/0126.htm.

Keenan, Elizabeth Angela, SND, trans. *The Fathers of the Church: St Cyprian Treatises*. Catholic University of America Press: 1958.

Manteau-Bonamy, H. M., O.P. *Immaculate Conception and the Holy Spirit*. Translated by Richard Arnandez, F.S.C. Franciscan Marytown Press, 1977.

Mark, Joshua J. "Enuma Elish: The Babylonian Epic of Creation." *World History Encyclopedia*. May 4, 2018. https://www.worldhistory.org/article/225/enuma-elish---the-babylonian-epic-of-creation---fu/.

Methodius of Olympus. *The Banquet of the Ten Virgins*. Discourse 1. New Advent. Accessed July 10, 2024. https://www.newadvent.org/fathers/062301.htm.

Metz, René. "La Consécration des Vierges dans l'Église Romaine." *Revue d'histoire de l'Église de France* 41 (1955): 205–206.

Mishnah Nazir. Sefaria. Accessed July 15, 2024. https://www.sefaria.org/Mishnah_Nazir.1.1?lang=bi.

Nectarios of Aegina. "Greek Byzantine orthodox chant: Agni Parthene." Performed by Petros Gaitanos. Posted January 22, 2019, by Adoration of the Cross. YouTube. https://www.youtube.com/watch?v=i-3h9TQ312c.

Newman, John Henry. "Jesus the Light of the Soul." In *Meditations and Devotions*. Edited by Rev. W. P. Neville. Newman Reader. Accessed August 22, 2024. https://www.newmanreader.org/works/meditations/meditations10.html.

Nickson, Chris. "The Life of an Anchoress." *The History Press*. Last updated July 21, 2020. https://thehistorypress.co.uk/article/the-life-of-an-anchoress/.

Philippe, Jacques. *In the School of the Holy Spirit*. Sceptre Publishers Inc, 2007.

Pitre, Brant. *Jesus and the Jewish Roots of Mary: Unveiling the Mother of the Messiah*. Image Publishing, 2018.

——. "The Thirty-Second Sunday of Ordinary Time, Year A." Catholic Productions. Accessed July 23, 2024. https://catholicproductions.com/blogs/mass-readings-explained-year-a/the-thirty-second-sunday-of-ordinary-time-year-a.

Pius XII. *Sacra virginitas*. Promulgated March 25, 1954. https://www.vatican.va/content/pius-xii/en/encyclicals/documents/hf_p-xii_enc_25031954_sacra-virginitas.html.

Polycarp of Smyrna. "Epistle to the Philippians." New Advent. Accessed July 10, 2024. https://www.newadvent.org/fathers/0136.htm.

Ratzinger, Joseph Cardinal. Homily, "Gift in the Church and for the Church" at the Consecration of a Virgin. Delivered March 25, 1988. https://diolc.org/wp-content/uploads/2019/05/50th-Anniversary_Material_rev_02JULY19.pdf.

Rite of Consecration of a Virgin Living in the World. May 31, 1970. https://diolc.org/files/consecratedlife/Complete%20Rite.pdf.

Scola, Angelo. "The Nuptial Mystery at the Heart of the Church." *Communio* 25, no. 4 (1998): 630–662.

Second Vatican Council. *Gaudium et spes*. December 7, 1965. Vatican.va. https://www.vatican.va/archive/hist_councils/ii_vatican_council/documents/ vat-ii_const_19651207_gaudium-et-spes_en.html.

——. *Lumen gentium*. November 21, 1964. Vatican.va. https://www.vatican.va/archive/hist_councils/ii_vatican_council

/documents/vat-ii_const_19641121_lumen-gentium_en.html.

"The Shema." My Jewish Learning. Accessed July 7, 2024. https://www.myjewishlearning.com/article/the-shema/.

Shiffman, Lawrence. *Reclaiming the Dead Sea Scrolls: The History of Judaism, the Background of Christianity, the Lost Library of Qumran.* Jewish Publication Society, 1994.

"Tefillin (Phylacteries)." My Jewish Learning. Accessed August 22, 2024. https://www.myjewishlearning.com/article/tefillin-phylacteries/.

"Text of the Shema Prayer in Hebrew and English." Chabad.org. Published by Kehot Publication Society. Accessed July 7, 2024. https://www.chabad.org/library/article_cdo/aid/706163/jewish/Text-of-the-Shema-Prayer-in-Hebrew-and-English.htm#lt=primary.

Thérèse of Lisieux. Letter to Abbé Maurice Bellière. June 21, 1897. https://carmelitequotes.blog/2021/03/28/therese-msc36v-audacity/.

United States Association of Consecrated Virgins. *Volume I: An Introduction to the Vocation of Consecrated Virginity Lived in the World.* United States Association of Consecrated Virgins, 2012.

——. "The Vocation Tree." USACV. Accessed August 3, 2024. https://www.secure.consecratedvirgins.org/the-vocation-tree.

Varden, Erik. *Chastity: Reconciliation of the Senses.* Bloomsbury, 2023.

Vermeersch, Arthur. "Virginity." New Advent. Accessed September 25, 2022. http://www.newadvent.org/cathen/15458a.htm.

West, Christopher. "Holy Week, The Week of the Bridegroom." Posted March 29, 2021, by Theology of the Body Institute. YouTube.. https://www.youtube.com/watch?v=HCpiXOIGVeA.

Wojtyla, Karol. *Love and Responsibility.* Translated by Grzegorz Ignatik. Pauline Books and Media, 2013.

About the Author

Erin Kinsella is a consecrated virgin of the Archdiocese of Ottawa and a cohost of *In the Thicket*, a podcast on suffering and hope. Although she grew up Catholic, Erin drifted from the Faith during her university years. While pursuing graduate studies in virology, she encountered the Lord's mercy during a period of intense suffering and experienced a powerful reversion to the Faith. She was blessed to work in youth, young adult, and campus ministry for more than twenty years. Erin was consecrated to a life of virginity lived in the world in 2019 on the feast of the Exaltation of the Holy Cross. She holds a master of theological studies from St. Augustine's Seminary conjointly with the University of Toronto, and she completed her thesis on the theology of the suffering body. Erin is a frequent speaker and writer on topics including suffering, the Theology of the Body, and consecrated virginity.

Sophia Institute

Sophia Institute is a nonprofit institution that seeks to nurture the spiritual, moral, and cultural life of souls and to spread the gospel of Christ in conformity with the authentic teachings of the Roman Catholic Church.

Sophia Institute Press fulfills this mission by offering translations, reprints, and new publications that afford readers a rich source of the enduring wisdom of mankind.

Sophia Institute also operates the popular online resource CatholicExchange.com. *Catholic Exchange* provides world news from a Catholic perspective as well as daily devotionals and articles that will help readers to grow in holiness and live a life consistent with the teachings of the Church.

In 2013, Sophia Institute launched Sophia Institute for Teachers to renew and rebuild Catholic culture through service to Catholic education. With the goal of nurturing the spiritual, moral, and cultural life of souls, and an abiding respect for the role and work of teachers, we strive to provide materials and programs that are at once enlightening to the mind and ennobling to the heart; faithful and complete, as well as useful and practical.

Sophia Institute gratefully recognizes the Solidarity Association for preserving and encouraging the growth of our apostolate over the course of many years. Without their generous and timely support, this book would not be in your hands.

www.SophiaInstitute.com
www.CatholicExchange.com
www.SophiaInstituteforTeachers.org